Typical and Atypical Child and Adolescent Development 3

Perceptual and Motor Development

This concise guide offers an accessible introduction to perceptual development and motor development from infancy to adolescence. It integrates insights from typical and atypical development to reveal fundamental aspects of human growth and development, and common developmental disorders.

The topic books in this series draw on international research in the field and are informed by biological, social and cultural perspectives, offering explanations of developmental phenomena with a focus on how children and adolescents at different ages actually think, feel and act. In this succinct volume, Stephen von Tetzchner covers key topics in perceptual development including: the theory of perceptual development, early and later development of vision, visual impairment, early perception of sound, the development of hearing throughout childhood and adolescence, the development of musical skills, hearing impairment, deafblindness, smell and taste. The section on motor development explores: theories of motor development, gross motor development, fine motor skills and atypical motor development.

Together with a companion website that offers topic-based quizzes, lecturer PowerPoint slides and sample essay questions, *Typical and Atypical Child and Adolescent Development 3: Perceptual and Motor Development* is an essential text for all students of developmental psychology, as well as those working in the fields of child development, developmental disabilities and special education.

Stephen von Tetzchner is Professor of Developmental Psychology at the Department of Psychology, University of Oslo, Norway.

T0346692

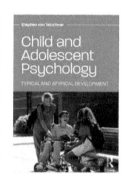

The content of this topic book is taken from Stephen von Tetzchner's core textbook *Child and Adolescent Psychology: Typical and Atypical Development*. The comprehensive volume offers a complete overview of child and adolescent development – for more information visit www.routledge.com/9781138823396

Topics from Child and Adolescent Psychology Series
Stephen von Tetzchner

The **Topics from Child and Adolescent Psychology Series** offers concise guides on key aspects of child and adolescent development. They are formed from selected chapters from Stephen von Tetzchner's comprehensive textbook *Child and Adolescent Psychology: Typical and Atypical Development* and are intended to be accessible introductions for students of relevant modules on developmental psychology courses, as well as for professionals working in the fields of child development, developmental disabilities and special education. The topic books explain the key aspects of human development by integrating insights from typical and atypical development to cement understanding of the processes involved and the work with children who have developmental disorders. They examine sensory, physical and cognitive disabilities and the main emotional and behavioural disorders of childhood and adolescence, as well as the developmental consequences of these disabilities and disorders.

Topics books in the series

Typical and Atypical Child and Adolescent Development 1
Theoretical Perspectives and Methodology

Typical and Atypical Child and Adolescent Development 2
Genes, Fetal Development and Early Neurological Development

Typical and Atypical Child and Adolescent Development 3
Perceptual and Motor Development

Typical and Atypical Child and Adolescent Development 4
Cognition, Intelligence and Learning

Typical and Atypical Child and Adolescent Development 5
Communication and Language Development

Typical and Atypical Child and Adolescent Development 6
Emotions, Temperament, Personality, Moral, Prosocial and Antisocial Development

Typical and Atypical Child and Adolescent Development 7
Social Relations, Self-awareness and Identity

For more information on individual topic books visit www.routledge.com/Topics-from-Child-and-Adolescent-Psychology/book-series/TFCAAP

Typical and Atypical Child and Adolescent Development 3

Perceptual and Motor Development

Stephen von Tetzchner

Routledge
Taylor & Francis Group

LONDON AND NEW YORK

Cover image: © Guido Mieth/Getty Images

First published 2023
by Routledge
4 Park Square, Milton Park, Abingdon, Oxon OX14 4RN

and by Routledge
605 Third Avenue, New York, NY 10158

*Routledge is an imprint of the Taylor & Francis Group, an
informa business*

British Library Cataloguing-in-Publication Data
A catalogue record for this book is available from the British Library

Library of Congress Cataloging-in-Publication Data
A catalog record has been requested for this book

ISBN: 978-1-032-27391-4 (hbk)
ISBN: 978-1-032-26771-5 (pbk)
ISBN: 978-1-003-29246-3 (ebk)

DOI: 10.4324/9781003292463

Typeset in Bembo
by Apex CoVantage, LLC

Access the companion website: www.routledge.com/cw/vonTetzchner

Contents

Introduction

Development can be defined as an age-related process involving changes in the structure and functions of humans and other species. Humans are complex beings who differ in various ways, with differences that are related to biology, experience and culture. Perceptual and motor abilities enable children to learn about and act on the world and hence are essential parts of development. The two parts in this topic book build on the models of development and the developmental way of thinking presented in Book 1, *Theoretical Perspectives and Methodology*. They include both typical development, which is the most common course, with unimpaired functions and ordinary individual differences between children, and atypical development, which represents various degrees of unusual or irregular development, including the development of children and adolescents who have perceptual or motor impairments. Children develop perceptual categories and strategies, and action strategies to master the physical and social world. Perceptual and motor skills are complementary in the development of exploration and understanding of the physical and social world. Perceptual difficulties may influence motor development and performance, and motor skills may influence the perceptual processes.

Human development to maturity stretches over about 20 years, and most individual differences in physical and mental features and abilities do not emerge directly from a particular biological or environmental factor but rather as a result of *interaction effects*, where biological and environmental factors are moderated by one or several other factors. Perceptual and motor abilities are shared by all humans, although there are individual differences, and some children have severe perceptual or motor impairments and never reach the skill level of their peers. Although perceptual and motor abilities have a strong genetic basis, experience still has an influence on their development. Development is never a one-way process: it is a *transactional process*, characterized by reciprocal influences between the child and the environment over time. Readers may find it useful to consult Book 1, *Theoretical Perspectives and Methodology*, or the corresponding chapters in the complete book before reading the present book.

The senses are the interface with the environment, and there is a complex sequence of processing from the stimulation of the sense organs to the perceptual experience. *Part I Perceptual Development* is about the sensory and perceptual processes that enable children to make sense of the environment and allow them to move around and act in it. Attention gives selectivity to perception. Perception includes the ability to distinguish between and identify sensory impressions, but adults do not see color surfaces and shapes, but meaningful entities such as houses, trees, humans, animals and chairs. They do not hear changes in frequencies but the baby screams, machine noises or language expressions derived from the acoustic patterns. It is thus not the physical sensory impressions in themselves but the meaning they are assigned and the categories children form from what they experience that change with development.

The genetic basis of the senses and perceptual processing is the result of evolutionary processes (phylogeny). The genes also contribute to individual differences in perceptual processing, for example in color vision or auditory acuity. The senses begin to function half way into the fetal period in the sheltered environment of the womb, with limited variation in sensory stimulation (see Book 2, *Genes, Fetal Development and Early Neurological Development,* Part II). However, the sensory experiences prior to birth are very different from those of more developed children, and post-natal perceptual development depends on varied sensory experiences. The senses are necessary for exploring the physical world and getting to know the perceptual characteristics of humans, animals, objects and locations – how they look, sound and feel. Perception makes it possible to identify people, objects and places and constitutes a basis for observational learning (see Book 4, *Cognition, Intelligence and Learning,* Chapter 35), observing regularities and contingencies, for example how people, things and sounds appear together and how different actions are performed.

The senses and the perceptual processes are built up in such a way that they promote interaction with other humans. The social interaction of the newborn period and the early preference for the mother's voice reflect the social nature of perceptual development. All communication and language modes have recognizable expressions, and perception is necessary for joint attention and comprehension of communication and language (see Book 5, *Communication and Language Development*). Even basic perception represents complex processing, but the ability to manage and make sense of complex sensory stimulation increases with age, including visual art and music. For children, the social interaction afforded by the early perceptual preferences contributes to the baby's survival, ensures help with challenges and is a source of learning. Insight into perceptual development is therefore central to understanding how people and human cultures work.

Sensory impairments can have a significant impact on children's learning (see Book 1, *Theoretical Perspectives and Methodology*, Chapter 30), but the other senses can be used to compensate for a functional loss due to severe impairment in one sense. In children with typical development, their vision enables physical recognition, but children who are blind can be guided to utilize hearing and touch to compensate for their lack of vision. Hearing is especially important for the perception of speech, but sign language is produced in a modality that makes language accessible for children who lack hearing. Letters are graphical figures which are usually read with eyes, but Braille letters are functionally equivalent to written letters and can be perceived with the tactile sense. However, when a child has significant congenital loss in both the distal senses – hearing and vision – compensation of functions will be extremely difficult.

Part 2 Motor Development is about the emergence of self-propelled mobility (gross motor skills), investigation and manipulation of objects (fine motor skills), and gradual learning to act on the world in different ways. Children go through a significant motor development in the first years of life, and this changes how they explore the physical and social world. Mobility has a broader impact on children's development than their just becoming able to move from one place to another. Exploration of people, places and objects is essential for children's understanding of their expanding physical and social environment. Self-propelled mobility increases children's range of actions and enables them to approach people and objects in the environment and to engage in play and other activities involving more advanced motor skills. It allows children to select what they want to explore to a greater extent. They may seek the familiar and safe, as well as new and unexplored objects and locations, learning to cope with new challenges and utilize the possibilities of their widening physical and social environment.

Independent mobility changes children's psychological space in a fundamental manner. Mobility implies the development of a broader repertoire of attachment behaviors, which enable the child to seek proximity and security, as well as safe exploration (see Book 7, *Social Relations, Self-awareness and Identity,* Part I). In the first months of life, when children's mobility is limited, parents tend to cheer all the child's attempts at moving. However, the greater range of action that follows from increased mobility also means that children more easily get near to traffic and other dangers. The increased risks make parents place new constraints on children's movements and actions. This may imply more conflicts between the child's wishes and the parents' need to ensure the child's safety.

Motor skills are implied in all aspects of life. Nearly all children acquire basic gross motor skills such as walking or running, and some develop extreme motor control and behavior, such as ski jumpers or competition dancers. Fine motor skills include throwing and catching balls, while sports such as tennis and bowling require coordinated gross and fine motor skills. Most children learn to draw, and some develop into creative artists. The motor skills also reflect what the child's culture finds important for children to learn, and that children learn to do things in the same manner as the people around them. Development of motor skills is therefore a foundation of the enculturation process.

The fact that most human activities require motor skills implies that severe motor impairments tend to have a significant impact on children's learning and development. Children with severe motor impairments may have to do ordinary actions in unusual ways or use assistive technology to compensate for their lacking motor functions, for example wheel chairs for self-propelled mobility, and to obtain attachment security. However, many actions take longer, hindering or limiting their participation in many ordinary children's activities. The result may be a smaller experiential foundation for development.

Perception and motor skills are closely related to cognition (see Book 4, *Cognition, Intelligence and Learning*). Perception is an integral part of cognitive development, and, except for where there is organic damage to the sensory apparatus itself, it is difficult to distinguish the processes of perception and cognition. Insights into the developmental possibilities and constraints presented by impairments in a child's sensory system or motor system can reveal a need for particular inter-vention measures. Habilitation and rehabilitation measures are based on the assumption that medical, educational and psychological mea-sures will change children's access to the environment in a broad sense and thereby moderate or prevent the negative developmental course that the impairments might imply without such measures. Knowl-edge of the issues presented in this topic book is therefore relevant for *applied developmental science*.

Some of the terminology used in developmental psychology may be unfamiliar to some readers. Many of these terms are highlighted and can be found in the Glossary.

Part I

Perceptual Development

I

Perception

Perception is the ability to distinguish and identify sensory information, to direct and sustain attention to various aspects of the environment and to lend meaning to them. Children use their senses to explore the physical and social world, to establish a basis for action and to monitor and regulate their own actions. The sensory systems facilitate interaction with other people early in life.

Vision, the sense that provides the majority of information about the environment, is the most studied among the senses. Hearing, too, is of major importance for a child's ability to adapt, and auditory development is described fairly thoroughly. To some extent, these two senses can compensate for one another in children with severe visual or hearing impairment. A severe reduction in both senses has major consequences for a child's **development**. Developmental changes also take place in the ability to smell, taste and feel by touch, and in the coordination of impressions from multiple senses.

Research has largely focused on children's early perception. This is owing to an interest in the biological and experiential foundations of human **cognition**, and the fact that sensory functions by and large become fully developed in the course of early **childhood**.

DOI: 10.4324/9781003292463-2

2

Two Theoretical Explanations

The two central theories within the study of perceptual development have mainly focused on vision. Key questions are how children learn to coordinate sensory information with their actions, and how action and perception relate to one another.

Piaget's Constructivism

According to Piaget (1952), perception of the outside world is constructed by the individual itself. Children primarily gain knowledge of the perceptual properties of materials and objects by performing actions on them in the broadest sense. Here, the term action does not merely include physical actions, but any type of internal (mental) or external behavior. For example, an object assumes the property "graspable" when a child grasps it with the hand. In this way, action turns into a perceptual property. Perception entails a progressively more precise understanding of physical reality. Children differ from adults in their perception of the world and only begin to perceive the world like an adult once they have developed the corresponding cognitive skills.

Gibson's Ecological Theory

According to Gibson (1979), perception involves an active search for information in the environment. Perception does not need to be constructed, as the **correspondence** between perceptual-cognitive structures and the properties of the outer world makes the information provided by sensory stimulation directly meaningful to infants.

DOI: 10.4324/9781003292463-3

Vision is designed for seeing, just as the fingers of the hand are designed for grasping.

A child's direct perception also incorporates a relationship between characteristics of the physical environment and any *possibilities for action*, referred to as "**affordances**" by Gibson. Unlike properties ascribed to the environment by the individual, an affordance is something "offered" by the environment and therefore depends on the environment as well as the organism. A surface, for example, may be perceived as "standable" or "walkable" based on the physical apparatus human beings use when they stand or walk, in the same way a surface is perceived as having a color (cats and many other animals do not have color vision). Even children who have just begun to walk seem to be able to differentiate between surfaces that are suitable for walking and those that are not (Gibson et al., 1987). "Graspability" is a property directly associated with what is being perceived. Thus, perception leads to action, the opposite of what Piaget's theory proposes.

Gibson's theory is called "ecological" because it is based on the correspondence between perception and the properties of the physical world. Different species perceive the world in different ways, and a particular possibility for action will only be valid for some species. A fly sees the ceiling as being "walkable." For a monkey, a tree is "climbable," but not for a horse. According to Gibson, the properties perceived by humans have been adapted to the species's ecological niche through evolution. As perception is a priori, it does not represent a developmental problem: children perceive the world directly in a human way because they are human beings. These views are in line with other evolution-based theories (see Book 1, *Theoretical Perspectives and Methodology*, Part II).

Comparison between the Two Theories

Gibson's theory is based on the assumption that children are born with significant perceptual skills that continue to evolve. Perception is "direct" because it does not involve drawing inferences or **learning**. Piaget's theory considers perception to be "indirect" because sensory stimulation is converted by **cognitive structures**, knowledge and expectation. Piaget acknowledges the innate quality of only a number of basic perceptual abilities, such as **reflexes** that ensure

adaptation to sensory stimulation (such as pupil contraction in bright light) and the ability to perceive movement and contrast and to distinguish between figure and ground. According to Gibson, the ability to perceive three dimensions lies fully formed in the dynamic flow of information from sensory stimulation. Whereas Piaget's theory assumes that perception is constructed by the child itself, Gibson's model is based on a process whereby children are able to perceive constantly new details using their visual sense. Yet Gibson's theory, too, incorporates clear connections between perception and action: an affordance is a relation between properties of the environment and the structure of children's actions. When children's motor skills improve, new affordances emerge. At first, the floor becomes "crawlable," followed by "walkable" once the child is able to walk. These affordances appear automatically through children's natural interaction with the environment.

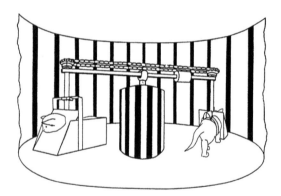

Figure 2.1 The importance of action in perceptual development.

Five pairs of kittens grew up with the same visual stimulation, but one kitten in each pair was able to move unrestricted, while the other sat in a gondola that was moved by the first kitten's movements. Subsequently, the kittens were placed on a bridge between a deep visual cliff on one side and a shallow part on the other. The kittens that had been able to move independently went down the shallow side, while the passive kittens just as often tried to climb down the deep side. Only the active kittens extended their paws when they were moved in such a way that they seemed to be about to collide with something. However, this need not be owing to a lack of depth perception, but could be owing to the fact that the kitten in the basket had learned that its movements had no influence on the actions surrounding it (**learned helplessness**) (Held & Hein, 1963, p. 873). (Copyright © 1963, American Psychological Association)

Although these two theories seem to stand in stark contrast to one another, it is not easy to design **experiments** that clearly differentiate between them, and arguments can be found in favor of both. Some species are born with well-developed perceptual skills, such as goat kids, which stay away from abysses right after birth. The perceptual skills that can be observed in early **infancy** (see the following sections) speak in favor of Gibson's theory. However, they do not furnish a sufficient basis to conclude that Gibson's affordance-based model is correct, but only that action and experience do not seem to be required for the development of perception to the extent argued by Piaget.

On the other hand, a classic experiment demonstrates the importance of autonomous action for the development of visually guided behavior. Held and Hein (1963) designed an experiment in which one kitten in a pair was able to move on its own and the other was a passive recipient of visual stimulation (Figure 2.1). The active kitten showed better perceptual development than the one sitting in the gondola. Thus, Held and Hein's study supports Piaget's assumption about the relationship between perception and action.

Assuming that perception and action mutually affect each other, the two theories may actually describe different aspects of the same process. According to Bremner (1997), the most important milestone in children's perceptual development is their ability to use perceptual knowledge to guide their actions and integrate sensory and action-related knowledge. Perception is neither as direct as Gibson claims, nor as dependent on action as Piaget assumes.

3

Vision

Vision is important for recognizing people, things and places in one's surroundings, and for monitoring and regulating one's own actions such as walking or reaching for something. It is commonly assumed that these two types of tasks are handled separately – that the *perceptual system* (the "what" system) and the *action system* (the "how" system) are in different parts of the visual **cortex** of the brain, that they develop relatively independently (the perceptual system before the action system) and that injury or abnormalities in the two systems will have different consequences (Dilks et al., 2008).

Early Development of Vision

The retina and the central visual system are still incomplete at birth, and full functionality of vision can only be acquired through experience. Objects are projected onto the retina in different ways, depending on light conditions and their location relative to the viewer. In order to experience the world as stable, children have to develop **constancy** and be able to disregard irrelevant variations. They must be able to perceive objects as being identical, independent of distance, angle, lighting conditions and so on. Piaget considers the acquisition of constancy to be one of the key factors in perceptual development (see Book 4, *Cognition, Intelligence and* Learning, Chapter 3).

Research has above all focused on visual acuity, perception of motion, object perception, depth perception, color vision and facial **recognition**. During the first year of life, children acquire basic skills, but the development of visual strategies continues all the way to adulthood.

DOI: 10.4324/9781003292463-4

Visual Acuity

For a long time it was believed that infants perceive very little of the world around them. William James (1890) referred to the perceptual experience of infants as "blooming, buzzing confusion." The view on infant competence was revolutionized when Fantz and his colleagues, in 1958, used a visual preference technique (see Book 1, *Theoretical Perspectives and Methodology*, Chapter 25) in connection with paired line patterns and white surfaces to examine the visual acuity of children a few months of age, that is, the spatial resolution of their visual system. The children spent more time looking at the lines than the white surface, meaning that they had to have sufficient visual acuity to perceive the lines. Since then, studies have

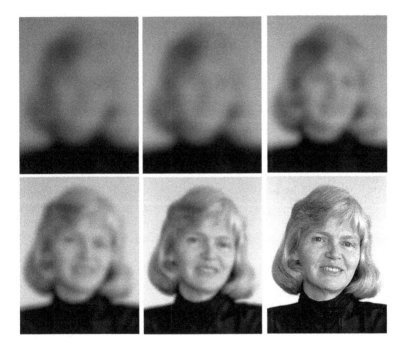

Figure 3.1 Visual acuity in children of different ages.

The photographs illustrate how newborns, children aged 1–2, 3 and 6 months, 2 years and adults perceive faces. The photographs have been produced using filters that simulate the visual process based on what is known about infant vision. (Photo: Tony Young)

shown that the visual acuity of newborn children is inferior to that of adults, partly owing to a smaller retina and a poorer ability to adjust the lens of the eye to distance and produce a sharp image (von Hofsten et al., 2014). Newborns do not see details, but they are able to perceive the outline of faces (see Figure 3.1) and larger movements. The optimal distance for infants to produce a sharp image is 20–40 centimeters. This is usually also the distance between the face of a newborn and an adult during interaction (von Hofsten, 1993). At 6 months of age, visual acuity has improved and, by the end of the preschool period, it is comparable to that of adults (Lewis & Maurer, 2005; Skoczenski & Norcia, 2002).

Movement

Infants are generally more aware of something that moves than something that is stationary. In one study, when infants were shown two similar patterns – one of them static, the other one moving – they looked twice as long at the moving patterns. They also habituated more rapidly to shapes they had previously seen in motion than to new objects. This shows that the infants had perceived the shape of the moving objects (Slater et al., 1985). In their first few months of life, infants become better at perceiving and following the movements of people and things with their eyes and begin to show that they expect an object disappearing behind a screen to reappear on the other side of the screen by anticipating the movement and moving their eyes to that side before the object has appeared (Rosander & von Hofsten, 2004).

Children must also be able to distinguish between visual changes caused by their own movements and those that result from the physical movement of objects, two situations that produce different types of visual information. When an object moves, it changes position relative to its background in a different way than when the observer moves (Britten, 2008).

Shape and Pattern

Studies based on visual preference show that newborns are able to distinguish between simple squares, triangles, circles and crosses, between patterns in which only the orientation of the lines differs (vertical and horizontal) and between sharp and blunt angles (Slater, 2001).

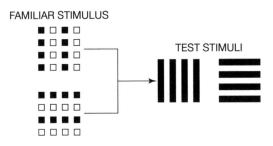

Figure 3.2 Early Gestalt organization of visual stimulation.

Three-month-olds seem to perceive black and white squares as a pattern. Those who had been shown horizontal rows of black and white squares spent more time looking at the vertical stripes, while those who had been shown vertical columns spent more time looking at the horizontal stripes; 5–6-month-olds – but not 3–4-month-olds – showed a similar preference for horizontal and vertical lines when the rows and columns consisted of circles and squares that the children had been habituated to (based on Quinn, 2006).

Children seem to organize visual impressions in line with **Gestalt principles**, where "similarity," "proximity" (grouping) and "good continuity" determine what is perceived to belong together. Three-month-olds perceive identically colored shapes as a pattern (Figure 3.2), and 6-month-olds organize rows and columns with identical shapes in a similar way (Quinn, 2006).

Children also develop a gradual preference for more complexity. One-month-old children look longer at eight large squares, while 2-month-olds spend more time looking at an equal-sized board containing 32 smaller squares (Fantz & Fagan, 1975). One-month-olds, however, do not seem to perceive square patterns and other visual patterns as a whole. They focus on a small part of the board, while 2-month-olds look at larger board areas.

Object Recognition

The world contains many objects, and to identify objects children must be able to perceive the *extent* of objects and the *boundaries* between them. A dog with a body, four legs, a head and a tail, for example, is *one* object, while a rider on horseback consists of two. In the first months of life, children have difficulty distinguishing the boundaries between objects. In one study, 3-month-olds did not seem to perceive two objects when one object was stationary within the boundaries of a larger object – such as a toy animal in a car – even when the toy animal's color and texture differed from those of the car (Kestenbaum et al., 1987). With increasing age, children make better use of various clues, but even 10–12-month-olds do not seem to perceive a toy animal in a toy car as two objects (Spelke & Newport, 1998; Xu & Carey, 1996).

Objects are rarely seen in isolation but are usually part of a larger "visual scene" in which they partially occlude other objects and in turn are partially occluded themselves, so that the objects' visual boundaries do not coincide with their actual physical limits. Studies indicate that children early on perceive a partially occluded object as a single unit if its visible parts move at the same time. The results of the study in Figure 3.3 suggest that the 4-month-old children perceived the object moving behind a block as one object. That they looked longer at the broken rod than the complete one was interpreted as indicating that the two pieces of broken rod were not expected by the children (Kellman & Spelke, 1983).

According to Spelke (1990), children are born with **core knowledge** about objects (see Book 1, *Theoretical Perspectives and Methodology*, Chapter 15), including an innate strategy that allows them to form an understanding of partially overlapping objects. This strategy does not include information about where one object begins and another ends, but *limits* the possible boundaries of objects and helps children form a more comprehensive and meaningful understanding of what they see. One problem with Spelke's theory however is that, in similar experiments, newborns looked longest at the complete rod, and 2-month-olds did not show any preference, but looked equally long at the complete rod and the broken rod. Thus, there seems to be a gradual development in the perception of objects (Slater, 2001). Shared movement appears to be an important clue, and infants quickly gain experience with moving objects. Nevertheless, Condry and associates (2001) argue that newborns cannot demonstrate their innate knowledge of objects because they still do not have the necessary perceptual skills. Other theorists believe that the perception of objects is governed by certain genetically determined factors, but that experience and learning play a more important role than assumed by Spelke (Johnson, 2004, 2005; Kagan, 2008). Thus, there continues to be considerable disagreement on the innate basis of object perception (see also Book 4, *Cognition, Intelligence and Learning*, Part III).

Habituation stimulus

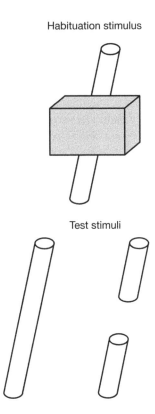

Test stimuli

Figure 3.3 Infant perception of partly occluded objects.

Four-month-olds were shown a rod that was partially occluded by a block until they became habituated (looked at it less often). In some of the experiments, the rod moved behind the block, at other times the block and the rod moved together. Then the children were shown either an entire rod or two smaller rods with a space between them. When the rod and the block were stationary during **habituation**, the children looked equally long at the complete rod as they did at the two pieces. When the rod had moved behind the block, the children looked longer at the two separate parts of the rod than at the complete rod (based on Kellman & Spelke, 1983, p. 508).

Size

Knowledge of the size of objects is important, as size determines what can be done with them. The image projected onto the retina represents a relative size however and depends on the distance between the eye and the object. Studies suggest that **size constancy** does not depend on experience but is present at birth. In one study, newborns first habituated to either a large or a small block. Then they were shown the same block, or a larger or a smaller block, but the distance between the child and the object was adjusted so that the object's projected size on the retina remained the same. The children spent more time looking at one of the differently sized blocks (**dishabituation**) than the one they had been shown during habituation. Thus, they were able to perceive a difference between the objects, even if the image on the retina remained the same, probably because the eyes focus differently at various distances (Kellman, 1996; Slater et al., 1990). The results suggest that children have an innate ability to integrate visual information on distance adaptation (**accommodation**) with information about the size of the retinal image. But development continues until **school age** before children acquire size constancy for objects located further away (Granrud & Schmechel, 2006).

Depth Perception

To orient themselves in a three-dimensional world children must become able to judge distance and to understand how objects are located and move relative to each other and themselves. Depth perception is based on **stereoscopic vision** and *pictorial depth cues.*

The distance between the eyes results in a small difference between the images projected onto each retina when the eyes are directed at the same point (hold a finger in front of your face and look at it with first the left eye closed, then the right one). When the brain combines these two images, space is perceived as three-dimensional. Children begin to develop stereoscopic vision at 3 months of age, and usually it is fully developed about 3 months later. When two appealing objects are placed at different distances from 5-month-olds, they will reach for both objects to an equal extent, regardless of whether they are viewing them with both eyes (binocular) or with one eye covered (monocular). Children who are 2 months older reach for the nearest object when viewing with both eyes, but equally for both when one eye is covered. This shows that they have developed the ability to exploit the difference between the images in each eye, or stereoscopic vision. This development is dependent on appropriate stimulation: both eyes must be stimulated equally and simultaneously before the age of 2. If the stimulation remains uncoordinated or if one eye is prevented from being used over a longer period during early development, children will not develop stereoscopic vision (Lewis & Maurer, 2005).

Pictorial depth cues, such as light, surface and relative height, provide cues to how objects are positioned relative to each other. For example, when objects partially or completely cover other objects located behind them in space, the latter appear to be located "above" the objects that are closer to the viewer. Children's use of such cues is based on experience and begins at the age of 5 months. The way in which children make use of different cues varies with each type of cue and shows greater **individual differences** than in connection with stereoscopic vision (Kavšek et al., 2009; Yonas et al., 2002).

In a classic experiment on depth perception in infants, Gibson and Walk (1960) built a table with a glass top and placed a checkerboard pattern underneath part of the glass plate to give the impression of depth (see Book 6, *Emotions, Temperament, Personality, Moral, Prosocial and Antisocial Development*, Box 0.0). Children aged 6–14 months who had begun to crawl or otherwise move independently were placed on the "shallow" part of the table and encouraged by their mother to come to her. When the mother was positioned in such a way that the children did not have to move beyond the apparent edge of the cliff, they quickly moved toward her. Only a few of the children moved toward their mother when they had to move past the visual cliff. The results suggest that children at this age are able to perceive depth and will try to avoid places that are too deep.

Depth perception is also important for the perception of size constancy – the ability to perceive changes in the size of an object that moves in space seems to develop at an early age. One-month-olds respond by blinking when an object appears to be approaching ("appears to be" because blinking may otherwise be a response to the air pressure caused by actual moving objects). At the age of 2 weeks, children raise their arms as if to protect themselves when a block seems to be approaching (Nanez, 1988). This suggests that children are able to perceive objects moving toward them at an earlier **stage** than they are capable of perceiving depth in general.

Color Vision

Color vision is somewhat incomplete at birth, but children aged 1–2 months are able to distinguish colors about as well as adults (Bornstein, 1992). Four-month-olds seem to categorize the color spectrum into the main categories blue, green, red and yellow, similar to the way adults do. The transitions between colors are less pronounced in infants, but the development continues, and, at 3–4 years of age, the boundaries between color categories have become clearly more distinct (Raskin et al., 1983).

Facial Perception

By the time a child is born, the visual system has developed in such a way that the infant is attentive to other people, especially their faces. Newborns prefer stimulation with curved lines, strong contrasts, varied edges, movement and complexity (Fantz & Miranda, 1975; Goren et al., 1975). The preference for faces temporarily disappears at 1 month of age and returns at around 3 months (Johnson et al., 1991; Turati et al., 2005). At this age, a change takes place in the processing of faces from the deeper parts of the brain to the cerebral cortex (Nelson et al., 2008). Figure 3.4 shows that infants look longest at images that resemble a face, but also that the characteristics of visual stimulation preferred by children change rapidly. This suggests that children have an innate preference not for faces as such, but for the typical features of many faces. Infants must learn to recognize faces but are initially aided by their preference for the type of complex stimulation faces convey.

Newborns are most attentive to the outer edges of the face. At 2 months of age, they begin to focus more on the central part of the face. At this age, parents usually report that their children begin to make eye contact. Eye movement tracking furthermore shows that 1-month-olds look at only a small part of the face, while 2-month-olds look at several parts. Children thus gradually develop a more comprehensive and detailed ability to perceive faces (Slater & Butterworth, 1997). Between the ages of 3 and 6 months, the ability to distinguish between different faces and facial expressions increases as well (see Book 6, *Emotions, Temperament, Personality, Moral, Prosocial and Antisocial Development*, Chapter 6).

Some theorists believe that infants' aptitude for recognizing faces suggests that humans have an innate **module** for facial recognition. According to Carey (1996), the way in which sensory stimulation is processed does not change – changes in facial recognition are solely the result of **maturation** and increased experience with faces. Other theorists believe that infants do not have a special ability to recognize

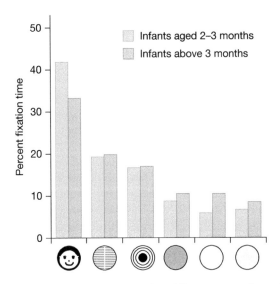

Figure 3.4 Viewing time of infants exposed to different types of stimulation.

In the first months of life, infants spend more time looking at patterned stimulation than at monochrome images and give most attention to faces and stimulation with facial characteristics (Fantz, 1961, p. 72).

faces, but that early facial recognition is the result of a general ability for perceptual learning. They point out that most people are "experts" on faces, and that some are experts on dogs, cars and other things as well. The ability to recognize faces is similar to other specialized forms of recognition, and faces are extremely prominent in an infant's environment and immediately gain importance through the interaction with caregivers. It is the human environment itself, with its prominence of voices and faces, that gives rise to specialized knowledge and furnishes the basis for what may appear to be a separate "mechanism" (Nelson et al., 2008; Slater & Butterworth, 1997). The "expert theory" is supported by the fact that children under the age of 4 months do not react differently to faces that are presented right side up or upside down. After this age, facial recognition becomes orientation-specific (Fagan, 1979).

During the first weeks of life, infants usually see their mother's face more than any other. The sound of her voice helps the child direct the gaze and learn to recognize her quickly (Sai, 2005). In one study, 5-day-old infants spent more time looking at their mother than at an unfamiliar woman, but this changed when the stranger put on a wig that matched the mother's hair, suggesting that children initially use the outline of their mother's head as a clue for recognition (Bushnell et al., 1989). Thus, children's earliest clues contain little detail, a natural consequence of infants' limited visual acuity. Gradually, the individual features of the face gain more importance, but the combination of contour and facial features always provides the best basis for recognition, also in adults (Want et al., 2003).

Studies show that infants typically recognize the faces of women better than those of men. In one study, 3–4-month-olds spent more time looking at female faces than male faces when they were presented in pairs. In another study, infants habituated (see Book 1, *Theoretical Perspectives and Methodology*, Chapter 25) to a female face and dishabituated when they were shown a different female face, but did not dishabituate when they were shown a different male face after having habituated to a male face. However, all of the infants had spent most of their time together with their mother. Similar studies involving infants who were mostly together with their father showed that they reacted the same way to male faces as the other children did to female faces (Quinn et al., 2002). This indicates that children's early experience with faces has significance for how they distinguish between faces.

Adults generally find it more difficult to distinguish between people from other races than those belonging to their own race. Early in life there is no such difference. Between the ages of 4 and 8 months, children begin to improve at recognizing people of their own rather than other races, no matter what race they belong to (Ferguson et al., 2009; Kelly et al., 2009). Six-month-olds are able to distinguish between races other than their own, while 9-month-olds seem to group all other races into a single category – "we" and "they" (Quinn et al., 2016). Children who grow up in homes with several races naturally do not show such differences (Bar-Haim et al., 2006). Kinzler and Spelke (2007) believe that humans have an innate core system (see Book 1, *Theoretical Perspectives and Methodology*, Chapter 15) to distinguish between "us" and "them," but this type of intrinsic mechanism is not required to explain facial recognition in infants. The results are entirely consistent with the general development of the perceptive system, as many areas undergo a *reduction* in the ability to **discriminate**.

Children's ability to distinguish between the characteristics of people, sounds and common objects in the environment is preserved, while the ability to distinguish between features that occur rarely, or not at all, disappears (Scott et al., 2007). This is part of the brain's tendency to "economize" and maintain systems for what is most common and familiar (see Book 2, *Genes, Fetal Development and Early Neurological Development*, Chapter 15).

Critical Visual Stimulation

The visual system has developed through evolution in a physical and human environment, so that growing up in a normal environment ensures the type of stimulation needed for normal development. A number of experimental animal studies have shown that visual stimulation early in life is necessary for the development of visual function. One study found that chimpanzees that had grown up in darkness during the first 16 months of life were able to respond to light, but could not differentiate between various visual patterns (Riesen, 1947). Under such conditions, the cells of the retina and the brain's visual cortex deteriorate owing to lack of use (atrophy). Studies show that atypical visual stimulation may result in a neurological organization that differs from the **norm**, such as when kittens grow up with either vertical or horizontal stripes only (Figure 3.5). The results show that the kittens' experiences affected the processing of visual information, as the brain can only process impressions based on some degree of prior experience and formation of the necessary nerve connections (see Book 2, *Genes, Fetal Development and Early Neurological Development*, Chapter 15).

Studies of children with illness or injury of the visual system have contributed important information about the development of vision. A **cataract** is a clouding of the eye's natural lens. The usual treatment is to remove the lens and replace it with an artificial one that creates a sharp image on the retina. When children whose vision was severely impaired owing to the illness during the first weeks or months of their lives were examined 10 minutes after removal of bandages, they showed the same visual acuity as newborns, regardless of whether they were 1 week or 9 months old. After only 1 hour, their visual acuity was equivalent to that of a 6-week-old child (Lewis & Maurer, 2005, 2009). This shows that visual acuity is not related to maturation alone, but also that its development requires little stimulation. At the age of

Figure 3.5 Growing up with vertical or horizontal stripes.

Kittens grew up in an environment with either vertical or horizontal stripes. The kittens that grew up with vertical stripes had difficulty perceiving horizontal stripes later on. The kittens that grew up with horizontal stripes had similar problems with vertical stripes (Blakemore & Cooper, 1970, p. 478. Reprinted with permission from *Nature*, Macmillan Magazines Ltd.).

6 months, the children's vision mostly fell within the normal range for this age group, but their visual acuity continued to be slightly reduced compared with that of their peers all the way into **adolescence**. The visual acuity of children who developed cataracts somewhat later and were left without the ability to see for a period of time was also impacted. Moreover, each eye develops relatively independently of the other, so that the vision of one eye is equally affected by a lack of stimulation regardless of whether the other eye is normal or not. In order to prevent one eye from taking over completely, children with strabismus and binocular vision problems therefore have to cover one of their eyes alternately with a patch.

The use of an eye patch ensures functional vision in both eyes

Later Development of the Visual Sense

Basic visual functions are established early on, and with increasing age children generally become faster, less distractible and more efficient at processing visual stimulation. In particular, the **integration** of various types of visual information undergoes a development. *Optical illusions* are a result of how the mature visual system organizes stimulation that consists of several different elements (Carbon, 2014). Children who are 4–5 years old *surpass* adults in judging whether two circles are of equal or different size when one of the circles is surrounded by larger or smaller circles (Figure 3.6). Adults are "fooled" by illusions because their visual system perceives different elements in context. As visual information is not yet fully integrated in children, they are less influenced by the elements that surround the circles they are comparing (Doherty et al., 2009; Káldy & Kovács, 2003). From the age of 7–8 years, their perception gradually approaches that of adults.

Studies have found that many people with **autism spectrum disorder** have particular problems with perception (Dakin & Frith,

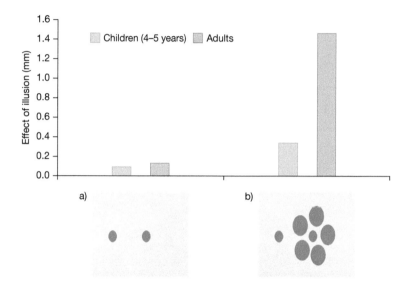

Figure 3.6 Perception of optical illusions in children and adults.

Children aged 4–5 years and adults were asked to judge whether two circles were equal or different in size. The two circles were shown (a) by themselves or (b) with one circle surrounded by circles of a different size. Adults were more influenced by the presence of visual elements surrounding the circle than children (Kovács, 2000, p. 1306).

2005; Simmons et al., 2009). Some, but not all, studies have found that they are less susceptible to optical illusions than others (Happé, 1996; Ropar & Mitchell, 2001). This suggests that the processing of visual stimulation is somewhat differently organized, and that the integration of perception in persons with autism spectrum disorder differs from that of other people.

The development of visual integration is also evident in children's perception of parts and wholes in drawings (see Figure 3.7). At age 6–11, children generally improve at differentiating and identifying visual information (Gibson, 1982). This development is related to issues involving vision, attention and other cognitive functions, but cultural differences also seem to play a role in the integration of visual elements. For example, adults in Japan are more susceptible to optical illusions than adults in the UK (Doherty et al., 2008).

Figure 3.7 Integration of visual information.

Children aged 4–9 years were asked to tell what they saw when presented with drawings such as the ones shown here. The answers were divided into parts, wholes and both (both parts and wholes for the same drawing). If the child did not mention either a part or a whole, they were asked once again whether they saw anything else. About 71 percent of children aged 4–5 years named parts only. The remaining responses consisted of wholes or both wholes and parts. Six-year-olds named parts about half of the time. Only at the age of 7 did parts account for less than half of the responses, and, even among 9-year-olds, 21 percent of the responses referred to parts only, without responding to wholes when they were asked if they saw anything else (Elkind et al., 1964, p. 84). (Permission granted by Elsevier)

Children improve at recognizing faces and facial expressions throughout childhood (Karayanidis et al., 2009). In one study, children aged 6–16 years were first shown 36 pictures of faces for 5 seconds each. Then they were shown the same pictures together with pictures of other faces and asked to point out the faces they had seen before. Six-year-olds were able to identify 70 percent of the faces, just above chance level, which would have resulted in

50 percent correct answers. Ten-year-olds identified 90 percent of the faces correctly. The same was true of 16-year-olds, while those aged 12–14 years were able to identify approximately 75 percent of the faces. One explanation is that the decline in recognition among the 12–14-year olds is related to maturation and the hormonal changes that occur during puberty (Carey, 1996). Another explanation is that adolescents begin to notice new features in other people's faces in connection with puberty, which is supported by the fact that they become better able to recognize faces of peers than those of adults (Picci & Scherf, 2016).

Pictorial Competence

An understanding of images (photographs, drawings, films, etc.) is a necessary skill in modern society. It entails the ability to recognize and lend meaning to what is depicted in an image or a film (e.g., a cat), and to understand that what is depicted corresponds to what exists in reality – that photographs and film can provide information about the environment, for example where something is located (Troseth et al., 2004).

Early Pictorial Competence

Children show early on that they are able to perceive what is depicted in an image, a form of recognition that probably requires little experience with images. With no little effort, Hochberg and Brooks (1962) raised their own son with minimal exposure to images until the age of 19 months. At this age, their son had acquired many words for objects and, when he was shown images of items that corresponded to these words, he was readily able to name them. In another study, 5-month-olds with normal pictorial experience were habituated to one of two different dolls and showed a preference for the other (new) doll, regardless of whether they were shown the actual doll or a picture of it. When they were shown a doll, a black-and-white photograph and a color photograph of it, they nonetheless looked longest at the doll (DeLoache et al., 1979; Slater et al., 1984). This suggests that infants are able both to recognize an object depicted in an image and to perceive that there is a difference between the object and the image.

Children's reactions to images change during early childhood. Nine-month-olds try to explore the objects in the pictures, while

15- and 19-month-olds vocalize and point. This is probably related to the fact that older children have developed new communicative skills, and that parents in many **cultures** like to point at pictures in books while talking to their children about them. Children also improve at using pictorial information. Eighteen-month-olds are able to use actions to show what happens in photographs and drawings, an ability that improves rapidly until the age of 30 months. Eighteen-month-olds are also more dependent on the realistic depiction of images. They show more actions based on photographs than drawings, whereas 24- and 30-month-olds show an equal number (Simcock & DeLoache, 2006).

An important aspect of pictorial competence is the relationship between the content of an image or a film and reality. This type of understanding develops long after the ability to recognize things on pictures. In one study, children aged 18–44 months saw an adult performing an action and were asked to point out which of three pictures corresponded to the action. One example was an adult splashing ketchup onto a toy pig. Each child was shown photographs of a clean pig, a pig with a white patch on its neck and a pig with a splash of ketchup and asked which of the pictures most resembled the pig. Despite the fact that the pig with ketchup stood right in front of the child, children below 2 years seemed to respond fairly randomly to the question (Harris et al., 1997).

In a series of studies, DeLoache and her colleagues surveyed children's use of pictorial information to locate an item, much like using a map. Children aged 24 and 30 months were shown photographs or drawings of a room in which a Snoopy dog or something else was hidden. The room included only a few furnishings that were easily visible in the pictures. In the first part of the study, the experimenter pointed to a location in the picture and said: *Snoopy would like to sit here. Can you go and put him there?* Seventy-five percent of the younger and all of the older children were able to perform this task. The next task was to find the Snoopy dog, which had been hidden by one of the experimenters. The experimenter pointed at the picture in which Snoopy was hidden, and almost all of the children approached the task with great enthusiasm, but only 13 percent of the 24-month-olds went straight to the correct location, whereas 72 percent of the children who were 6 months older were able to do so (DeLoache & Burns, 1994). This suggests that a major change takes place in children's ability to use graphical representations between the ages of

24 and 30 months, a result that may partly be explained by the fact that older children have been mobile for longer and are more familiar with exploring the environment. Studies using videos have led to similar results. Despite being given instructions and help, fewer than half of the 24-month-olds were able to use the information in a video to find a toy, whereas nearly 80 percent of the 30-month-olds achieved this task. When 2-year-olds could observe through a window that the experimenter was hiding a toy, all of them went straight to the toy, and over 60 percent managed to do so after looking through a "video window" (Deocampo & Hudson, 2005; Troseth & DeLoache, 1998). Studies have also shown that children under the age of 3 are unable to use a model of a room to find an item (Figure 3.8), about 6 months later than in the case of images (DeLoache, 1987; Troseth et al., 2007). Compared with images, toddlers seem to have relatively more difficulty understanding that a physical model represents something other than itself.

These studies show that children recognize objects in images and on video early on, and that they can name the items without any particular previous experience once they are able to talk. It takes some time for them to understand that there may be a direct relationship between an image and reality. In studies involving 2–3-year-olds, the children were startled to see themselves on video and were often unable to recognize themselves. For instance, they did not react to the fact that photographs or videos taken a few moments earlier showed that

Figure 3.8 A 3-year-old observes the experimenter hiding a small frog in a model of the room and finds a large frog in the "real" room (photographs courtesy of Judy DeLoache).

they had a sticker on their head, put there by the experimenter without their knowledge (see also Book 7, *Social Relations, Self-awareness and Identity*, Box 00.0). Four-year-olds reacted immediately by reaching for the sticker (Povinelli et al., 1999). One possible reason for this may be that most videos watched by children have nothing to do with themselves, but rather have to do with a fantasy world far removed from everyday life. When the families of a number of 2-year-olds connected a camera to their TV so the children were able to see their parents, siblings, pets and themselves on television for 2 weeks, they became as proficient at using the information on video as other 2½-year-olds (Troseth, 2003). The widespread use of digital cameras with instant viewing possibilities has probably allowed many of today's children to form an earlier understanding of the relationship between image and reality.

Later Development of Pictorial Understanding

Children's ability to perceive drawings as well as their preferences change throughout childhood. Toddlers prefer clear and unambiguous images, but also complexity and strong contrasts. Preschool children prefer bright colors, without regard to realism. Until the age of 7–8, distinctness is the most important requirement, while the demand for realism becomes stronger toward the age of 14 (Holm & Thau, 1984).

Also, the perception of detail undergoes a development during school age. At first, children generally see only the main motif or figure in a picture and only later develop the ability to perceive the background. Children's understanding of pictorial content also develops quite slowly. Constable and associates (1988) found that students all the way up to the first year of middle school had trouble understanding the illustrations and pictures in their biology textbooks, all of which were designed to make it *easier* to absorb the material. This may indicate that many of the illustrations used in textbooks are not well enough adapted to children's pictorial understanding and thus do not provide the educational benefits they potentially could (Carney & Levin, 2002; Cook, 2008).

Visual Impairment

Many children have a visual impairment that is easily corrected with glasses but may be difficult to detect at an early age. After all, children have no way of knowing that others see better than they do. Therefore it is important for all children to undergo an eye examination.

Severe visual impairment affects all areas, but blind children with no additional problems generally show relatively normal cognitive and language development. Owing to their difficulties with orientation and mobility, these areas are central to early intervention for visually impaired children (Kesiktas, 2009). Their motor development is typically somewhat delayed, probably because they cannot move with the same confidence as other children and because they lack the incentive for locomotion and **exploration** of the environment provided by visual impressions (Fazzi et al., 2002). During early development, blind children can often be passive, with little mobility and a tendency to listen and explore with their ears. It is difficult for them to perceive things at a distance, and it takes some time before they begin to reach for the source of a sound. Tactile exploration is initially limited to what they are able to reach (Fazzi et al., 2011), and they spend little time playing with objects. **Constructive play** is more limited, and they prefer toys that produce sounds, household items and common objects in their surroundings (Pérez-Pereira & Conti-Ramsden, 1999; Webster & Roe, 1998). Compared with sighted children, many everyday skills such as drinking from a regular cup, pouring liquid into a cup or building towers with Duplo bricks are acquired later (Brambring, 2007).

Blind children use human and other sounds to orient themselves. They may say the names of others, for example when playing in kindergarten, in order to discover who is there and where they are located. Their lack of overview leads to lower participation in many activities and also impacts social functioning. In addition, many blind children and adolescents need time to develop a mental map in order to navigate independently in familiar surroundings. This can inhibit participation in ordinary child and adolescent activities (Salminen & Karhula, 2014).

Blind and severely visually impaired children can access emotional information through sound, but **social referencing** can be difficult in many situations because they do not always fully comprehend the situation and the connotations of emotional words or expressions. They express joy and anger early on, but have a smaller repertoire of emotional expressions (Tröster & Brambring, 1992). Because their social smile is more uncertain and less frequent (see Book 6, *Emotions, Temperament, Personality, Moral, Prosocial and Antisocial Development,*

Chapter 6), parents can be affected in their reactions and interactions with the child. During the earliest developmental period, parents can feel rejected when their child does not turn its head toward them, rather than seeing it as an expression of the child's effort to concentrate and listen. They may react with disappointment and withdraw instead of establishing interaction. Parents need help to understand the inner world of their child, which is why guidance to parents and a "redefinition" of the child's actions are particularly important (Fraiberg, 1977; Sameroff, 2009).

Despite the lack of visual information, blind children engage in joint attention (see Book 5, *Communication and Language Development*, Chapter 2) and show a relatively normal language development, although many words have a somewhat different conceptual content and usage for them than for sighted children. When blind children say they want to "look at" something, they do not refer to vision, but to experience in a more general sense (Landau & Gleitman, 1985). They may confound "I" and "you" – words whose reference changes depending on who is talking (Pérez-Pereira & Conti-Ramsden, 1999). Nonetheless, language is the main source of information about social factors and the physical world, and early language skills are one of the strengths of many blind children.

The demands on children vary through development. Toward the end of **preschool age**, for example, many activities involve a great deal of running and moving about. During this period, children with visual impairments can lag behind, drop out from play and become passive because they are unable to follow the changes in activity and cannot move fast enough. Once they start school, the number of stationary activities increases, and they can choose friends and join groups of children who are more verbally oriented and not as physically active. Parents of blind children are often overprotective. During later school age, children with severe visual impairment are often passive and suffer from low **self-esteem** (Hodge & Eccles, 2013; Roe, 2008).

Many children with severe visual impairment have a number of other disorders, particularly motor impairments, auditory impairments and intellectual disabilities, and may need extensive support and adaptive measures (Geddie et al., 2013). The **incidence** of autism spectrum disorder among children with severe visual impairment is often rated to be high, and some believe that these children develop pragmatic disorders, problems with **mind understanding** and autism-like conditions because they are unable to observe other people's interactions and emotional reactions (Hobson & Bishop, 2003). Others are critical of these claims and believe that blind children's use of language must be understood based on their particular experience of the world (Pérez-Pereira, 2014).

Many children with disabilities are able to perceive visual impressions, but have trouble processing sensory input. Although there is considerable variation, ranging from slight impairment to near functional blindness, it is always important to assess and account for any possible disturbances in visual perception in connection with intervention and adaptive strategies for children with more extensive **developmental disorders** (Zihl & Dutton, 2015). Juvenile neuronal ceroid lipofuscinosis (**Batten disease**) is a neurodegenerative disorder involving the gradual loss of vision and, eventually, cognitive and motor skills as well. Such children require an altogether different type of developmental support and environmental adaptation than children with visual impairments who show a slow but positive development (von Tetzchner et al., 2019).

4

Hearing

Children explore the auditory environment with their ears just as they explore the visual environment with their eyes. Hearing is used to analyze "auditory scenes," listen to speech and to identify and locate people, things and events (Werner et al., 2012). The perception of speech sounds is especially important and will be described in Book 5, *Communication and Language Development*, Part 6, in connection with language development.

Early Perception of Sound

At birth, the development of hearing has progressed further than vision and dominates children's attention during the first few months of life (Robinson & Sloutsky, 2004). However, the peripheral auditory system (outer and inner ear) is more developed than the central auditory system, and a significant development has yet to take place in the brain's processing of auditory information (Morrongiello, 1990). Children are able to recognize and distinguish between sounds early on but need varied experiences to be able to process sounds and understand their meaning (Werner, 2007).

Studies based on habituation and **conditioning** show that newborns are able to distinguish between all aspects of acoustic stimulation but require higher audio levels and greater differences. While they show little reaction to sounds below 55–60 decibels (dB), above this level their reaction increases with the *intensity* of the sound (Steinschneider et al., 1966). At 1 month of age, the threshold lies 35 dB above that of adults (at 4,000 Hertz, Hz) and at 6 months 15 dB above. In addition to a certain intensity, sounds must also have a

DOI: 10.4324/9781003292463-5

minimum duration of 1 second in order to create a reaction in young infants (Johnson & Hannon, 2015).

Similarly, a gradual development occurs in the ability to distinguish between tones of different *pitch*. Three-month-olds react to differences greater than 120 Hz at around 4,000 Hz, a difference of 3 percent. Adults are able to notice a difference of 40 Hz, or 1 percent (Olsho et al., 1987). Six-month-olds react to differences in frequency from 1.5 to 3 percent, depending on the pitch (Trainor & He, 2013). Children's perception of sound is less detailed than that of adults, and they also have greater difficulty detecting a tone against a background of sound (auditory figure-ground), even if the background frequencies do not lie within the same bandwidth as the tone (Leibold, 2012).

Human Voices

Attention to voices is important for social orienting and creating affective ties between children and caregivers. A female voice saying "baby" elicits more motor activity in 3–8-day-old infants than pure tones (Hutt et al., 1968). Studies also show that newborns are especially sensitive to their mother's voice right after birth. When sucking on a pacifier is followed by the sound of a voice, children suck more when they hear their mother's voice than any other voice (Fifer & Moon, 1995). In a survey of 2-day-old children of English- and Spanish-speaking mothers, the children sucked more on the pacifier when they heard their mother's language. It is possible that the children remembered and recognized certain voice properties from their time in the womb, but, as they were exposed to their mother's language during the first 2 days, their preference may be due to early exposure and learning. Not all speech is equally interesting however. Children aged 2–4 weeks preferred their mother's voice when she spoke with the exaggerated **intonation** typical of adults talking to children, but not when she read the words of a text backwards, resulting in a monotonous tone of voice (Mehler et al., 1978). This suggests that intonation is important for recognition.

Localization

Sound is an important cue to the localization of people and things, and hearing enables children to find things that produce sound, such as identifying the source of a familiar voice. The brain localizes sounds by using the minute time and phase differences between each ear when a sound is heard. Newborn babies can roughly distinguish between left, right and straight ahead. Only a few hours after birth, children turn their heads to the right or to the left, depending on where the sound comes from (Wertheimer, 1961). The reaction disappears after about 6 weeks but returns at 3 months of age. This pause in development suggests that the turning of the head toward the sound, like many other early skills, changes from a primarily reflexive reaction to a voluntary response. At around 3 months of age, the movement toward sound also begins to be accompanied by visual exploration. In early infancy, children smile at the sound of their mother's voice alone; 3-month-olds do not smile until they see the face of their mother (see Book 6, *Emotions, Temperament, Personality, Moral, Prosocial and Antisocial Development*, Chapter 6). At 6 months, children show a noticeably greater interest in sounds accompanied by interesting visual stimulation, such as a brightly colored music box. They have learned more about the connection between sounds and their sources, such as humans, animals and other things, and sounds have become more meaningful to them. Nevertheless, it is not until the end of the first year of life that auditory and visual localization seem to be fairly well integrated (Neil et al., 2006).

The Development of Hearing throughout Childhood and Adolescence

In many areas, children approach adults in their ability to distinguish between sounds as early as infancy, but generally distinguish higher frequencies better than lower ones. Their ability to differentiate between the intensity of lower-frequency sounds continues to develop until the age of 10 (Johnson & Hannon, 2015).

At around 18 months, children can locate an isolated sound almost as precisely as adults under good acoustic conditions, but do not do equally well in noisier environments. Five-year-olds have significantly greater problems localizing a sound than adults in somewhat more complex sound environments such as a busy street, a room full of people or when the radio and television are turned on (Trainor & He, 2013). They also have more difficulty analyzing auditory scenes, separating sounds, identifying and localizing sounds when there are several people or things that produce sound, and when sounds change and partially coincide in time. The perception of auditory figure-ground remains difficult all the way into adolescence (Leibold, 2012).

Until the age of 10, children continue to be more affected by noise and irrelevant sounds. Older children and adults are more selective in their perception of sounds in the environment. Younger children's auditory attention is less affected by expectations, and they filter out relevant information to a lesser degree than adults (Werner, 2007). Thus, hearing shares many of the same developmental characteristics as vision.

Hearing Impairment

Congenital or early acquired hearing impairment has developmental consequences for the ability to orient oneself and explore the environment, as well as for social awareness, **communication** and language. However, the impact on various developmental areas is the result not merely of the hearing loss itself, but equally of how the environment is adapted to compensate for the lack of hearing, particularly in regard to language and social factors (Lederberg et al., 2013; Mitchell & Karchmer, 2004). Studies have documented that early detection along with appropriate measures for both child and family are important to ensure an optimal development (Yoshinaga-Itano, 2013). Lack of visual communication early in life, before the child's hearing may be restored, can result in fewer resources for other developmental tasks and make later language acquisition more difficult.

A key question has been how to best support the development of communication and language in children with severe hearing impairments. Hearing loss can be detected early (Lang-Roth, 2014), and it is possible to improve the perception of speech sounds, support the development of visual forms of communication and combine these two measures (see Book 5, *Communication and Language Development*, Chapter 11). High-quality hearing aids are available for mild-to-moderate hearing impairments, and in many countries deaf and severely hearing-impaired children can get a cochlear implant that converts sound into electrical impulses that are sent directly to the inner ear. Many children with severe hearing impairments use these hearing aids (which are not suitable for children with milder hearing loss) to good advantage and are able to function on the level of moderate hearing impairment, while they are deaf without the hearing aid. For best results, children have both ears operated on before the age of 18 months (van Wieringen & Wouters, 2015) and are followed up with visual support and various forms of training (Yoshinaga-Itano, 2013). Nevertheless, most of them are delayed in their speech development and have problems understanding and producing more complex utterances (Geers et al., 2009). Children (and adults) with cochlear implants also have greater difficulty perceiving **emotions** in the voice than children without hearing loss (Chatterjee et al., 2015).

Even a minor hearing loss can affect the ability to acquire spoken language (Spencer & Marschark, 2010). Both speech and common auditory scenes involving a number of people and background noise can result in a lack of clarity and be more difficult to analyze for children with hearing impairments (van Wieringen & Wouters, 2015). Some children have good hearing in only one ear, a fact that is often discovered late. It may influence orientation and attention, and studies show that children with hearing loss in one ear tend to have delayed language development, educational difficulties and an increased **prevalence** of behavior disorders (Lieu et al., 2012).

For some children, cochlear implants do not function well. Because it is impossible to know in advance to whom this may apply, children with hearing impairments should always be followed up in different ways (van Wieringen & Wouters, 2015). Bilingual competence in spoken and **sign language** in the child's environment is an important element of optimal language support (Becker & Erlenkamp, 2007). A shared language is important for the child's cognitive and emotional development. As only 5 percent of all deaf children have deaf parents, most parents with a deaf child need training and guidance (Lederberg et al., 2013). Children who use visual communication or need visual support must alternate between looking at the person they communicate with and the particular aspect of the situation they are communicating about. Deaf parents have experience with visual communication, whereas hearing parents must receive help to develop good visual strategies in communicating with their deaf child. Unlike deaf children with deaf parents, those with hearing parents are delayed in solving **theory of mind** tasks (see Book 4, *Cognition, Intelligence and Learning*, Chapter 23).

Children with relatively severe hearing impairments also need ergonomic support to allow their vision to compensate for the lack of hearing. In kindergarten and school, this involves creating good acoustic conditions and correct placement in relation to light and overview of the room. When children with unilateral hearing loss try to turn toward the sound in order to listen with their good ear, this can be perceived as restlessness and give rise to conflicts, for example during circle time when the child is positioned in the circle with the good ear facing out. This group of children benefit from attending small classes and seating in the classroom so the good ear faces away from noise (Kuppler et al., 2013).

Severe hearing impairment in itself does not lead to cognitive defects. Deaf children without other disorders receive normal scores on nonverbal cognitive **tests** (Spencer & Marschark, 2010). However, a large minority have additional disorders (see Book 1, *Theoretical Perspectives and Methodology*, Chapter 30). Language disorders also occur in deaf children, and some show signs of delayed language development (Woll & Morgan, 2012). Many hearing-impaired children have difficulty learning written language, among both those using sign language and those with hearing aids, but there is considerable variation depending on the general environment and the quality of the reading instruction (Lederberg et al., 2013). This is of great importance to their entire education.

Sound can direct a child's visual attention toward specific events. The loss of hearing can affect situational awareness and social participation, and communication with peers outside the home is often difficult. The incidence of **mental disorders** is higher in children with hearing impairments than in children with normal hearing (Stevenson et al., 2015). Hard-of-hearing children seem to be more vulnerable than deaf children, perhaps because they are expected to perform as well as others. People in the surroundings may pay little attention to the major and minor difficulties that hearing impairment always brings with it, making it difficult for hearing-impaired children to find an **identity** as either a deaf or a hearing person (Spencer & Marschark, 2010).

Deafblindness

The consequences of early deafblindness are exceptionally severe because tactile and haptic information cannot compensate for more than a small part of the information loss from the two most important senses during development. Although the consequences are major, they are far less severe once language (sign or spoken) has been acquired and merely needs to be translated to another modality such as tactile signing or Braille. The time at which deafblindness presents is therefore of great importance. Among others, Helen Keller and Laura Bridgeman lost their ability to see and hear at about 1½ years of age (see Fukushima, 2011), and their early communicative experiences may have been crucial for their positive development. Children with *precommunicative deafblindness* have difficulty establishing **joint attention**, and their lack of social experience limits their language development. The number of deafblind children is low, but an optimal development depends on a physical and social environment that is completely adapted to each child, in addition to individualized and intensive instruction and other measures (Nafstad & Rødbroe, 2016; Vervloed et al., 2006).

Development of Musical Skills

Musical ability is usually regarded as a separate area of development. Gardner (1993) believes musicality to be a unique form of intelligence, but most authorities consider musicality to be a type of ability other than intelligence (see Book 4, *Cognition, Intelligence and Learning*, Chapter 25). Unusual musical abilities are also found in people with severe learning disabilities or developmental disorders (Miller, 1989). Studies of people with congenital or acquired impairment in the ability to differentiate pitches and recognize melodies show that there is no connection between musicality and language ability. Children who have difficulty recognizing melodies or hearing that melodies are played incorrectly have no problems perceiving differences in the intonation of speech (Peretz & Hyde, 2003).

Studies on the development of musicality have particularly focused on the ability to distinguish between and produce pitched tones and melodies. Musicality undergoes a development from the perception and production of simple to more complex pitch patterns (see Table 4.1).

Perception of Music and Singing

Starting at an early age, children seem to react selectively to music and recognize short melodies and tone patterns. They also seem to

Table 4.1 Milestones in musical development (age ranges are approximate)
(Hargreaves, 1986)

Age (years)	
0–1	Respond to sound
1–2	Make up music spontaneously
2–3	Begin to reproduce parts of songs they have heard
3–4	Perceive a general outline of the melody May develop perfect pitch if they learn an instrument
4–5	Are able to distinguish between pitches and tap out simple rhythms they have heard
5–6	Understand high and low and are able to differentiate between simple pitch patterns and rhythms (similar/dissimilar)
6–7	Sing more in tune. Perceive tonal music better than atonal music
7–8	Prefer consonance to dissonance
8–9	Keep a steadier rhythm
9–10	Perceive the rhythm and remember the melody better. Perceive two-part melodies; have developed a sense for cadences (conclusion of a phrase or melody)
10–11	Establish a sense of harmony and appreciate more subtle musical aspects
12–17	Increasingly appreciate music and show a more sophisticated cognitive and emotional response

perceive melody constancy early on, as a pattern independent of the key (Chang & Trehub, 1977). Hearing forms the basis for melodic recognition, and musical perception is enculturated early on. Six-month-olds dishabituated equally to an incorrect note in melodies based on Western (major and minor) and Javanese musical scales, while 1-year-olds (as well as older children and adults) from Western cultures did better at Western scales (Lynch & Eilers, 1992). Six-month-olds were also better at perceiving music based on foreign scales than adults. This suggests that children begin with an unbiased ability to recognize melodies based on different scales and lose the ability to recognize scales they are not exposed to. Thus, there seems to be a development from melodic perception based on general auditory characteristics to culture-specific musical perception without any special training. This is similar to the process of recognizing speech sounds (see Book 5, *Communication and Language Development*, Chapter 6). Toward the end of preschool age and the start of school age, children begin to master many aspects of music. An understanding of harmony and more complex melodies, however, is first acquired during adolescence. Music education and other forms of musical experience are important for this development (Trainor & Unrau, 2012).

There is considerable disagreement about children's preference for *consonant* rather than *dissonant* melodies. Some experts argue that this is an innate ability, and that infants have a "built-in" sense for consonance (Masataka, 2006; Trainor & Unrau, 2012), but this is contradicted by Plantinga and Trehub (2014) who found a preference for familiar music rather than consonance in 6-month-olds (Box 4.1). They point out that preference is chiefly an expression of recognition, and that consonance is culturally determined. Children's preferences become clearer toward the end of preschool age, and there are major changes in musical perception up to the end of school age and an increasing preference for consonance and aversion to dissonance. Five-year-olds, for example, can detect incorrect notes outside a scale, but not within a scale, which 7-year-olds and adults are able to do (Trainor & Trehub, 1994). This development occurs earlier and is more pronounced in children with relatively good musical abilities (Winner, 2006).

Around the age of 1 year, some children begin to stamp their feet and move their hands up and down when they hear music, and, by 18 months, such motor reactions are common (Moog, 1963). At the age of 2 years, children are able to tap rhythms with their hand with about 21 percent accuracy, and almost 50 percent at the age of 5. A significant improvement in rhythmic perception occurs between the ages of 5 and 11. Adults have a rhythmic accuracy rate of about 87 percent (Hannon & Johnson, 2005; Jersild & Bienstock, 1935).

Children of all cultures are generally exposed to music from an early age, especially by adults who sing for them (Trehub & Schellenberg, 1995). Songs for infants are usually simple and emotive, with a leisurely tempo, a falling melodic line and repetitions of the same pattern. They are also sung in the same mode (major, minor, etc.) every time. Infants are more attentive to songs sung in this child-oriented

Box 4.1 Attention to Consonant and Dissonant Music in 6-Month-Olds (Plantinga & Trehub, 2014)

The attention of 64 infants aged 6 months was directed to a loud-speaker with flashing lights, and music was presented as long as the infants looked at the loudspeaker. When they looked away, the music stopped; the infant's gaze at the loudspeaker thus maintained the music. The figure shows that the infants looked slightly longer at dissonant than at consonant music, but the differences were not significant. In another experiment, the children were first exposed to 3 minutes of either consonant or dissonant music. When using the same procedure as in the first experiment, the infants looked longer at the loudspeaker that played the music they had heard just before, independent of consonance.

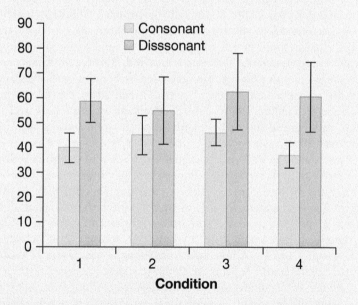

Mean cumulative looking time (seconds) at consonant and dissonant stimuli in each of four pairwise tunes. The bars represent standard errors, which indicate the variation in distribution of responses.

way than to the same songs when sung in a conventional way, as well as to songs at a higher rather than lower pitch (Winner, 2006). It has been argued that certain types of music (especially Mozart) have a positive effect on intellectual development, especially the ability to solve tasks that require good spatial perception (Hetland, 2000; Rauscher & Hinton, 2006; Rauscher et al., 1993). Belief in the "Mozart effect" has led to large sales of "intelligence-enhancing" music for parents who wish to stimulate their children's intellectual development, even during pregnancy. However, studies of children who have listened to Mozart and other types of music have not found evidence of such an effect (McKelvie & Low, 2002; Waterhouse, 2006a, b). Children's own music-making has a better effect (Trainor & Unrau, 2012).

Production of Songs and Music

Children begin to react to music early on by producing song-like sounds or moving to rhythms (Simons, 1964). Some children begin to make "**babbling** songs" by vocalizing at different pitches around the age of 6 months. At 9 months, the majority of children produce such babbling songs. At 1½–2 years of age, children begin to produce songs with a certain similarity to the songs sung for them by adults, and, from 2 to 5 years, spontaneous singing undergoes a development from simple to more complex "melodies" (Werner, 1961). Older preschoolers spontaneously sing children's songs and fragments of pop songs. When somewhat older children are asked to sing back simple songs, they make more mistakes in the most complex songs. Throughout childhood, the number of mistakes decreases, and children progressively improve at singing melodies correctly and in more detail. Practice has a significant effect but, in younger preschoolers, it merely leads to an improvement in the direct **imitation** of melodies. Children's spontaneous singing does not change, and practice first has an actual effect on their singing once they approach school age. The age at which children start singing melodies correctly varies considerably, and some never acquire this ability (Søbstad, 1974).

Individual Differences

Musical ability varies greatly from one child to the next. Often – but not always – several members of the same family share a high level of musical skill, as in the case of J. S. Bach's family. Outstanding musicians and singers have musical parents more often than others. For example Jussi, Rolf and Raymond Björling are three generations of opera singers. Although musicality undoubtedly involves biological factors, the prevalence of musicality within a family may just as well be the result of social influences. Twin studies suggest that there is a certain genetic basis, but that the contribution of genes is moderate (Shuter-Dyson & Gabriel, 1981). Howe and colleagues (1998) conclude that individuals who become prominent musicians do not seem to have a special innate talent compared with musicians in general, but that it is the amount of practice that distinguishes this group from others. Both special and more ordinary musical abilities depend on certain biological prerequisites, but the development of musicality also requires an environment that provides experiences and promotes the development of these skills.

5

Other Senses

Observations of everyday life show that newborns respond differently to various forms of *tactile* stimulation. They cry when they receive a vaccine shot and calm down when gently stroked on the back. Knowledge about the development of tactile perception is limited, but early in life the mouth is sensitive to tactile stimulation, and infants tend to explore objects with their mouths. The use of the mouth gradually decreases during the second half of the first year, and manual exploration increases (Ruff, 1984).

Smell

The sense of smell plays an important role in identifying people and food and is already well developed at birth (Monnery-Patris et al., 2009). Children are able to recognize different odors early on and prefer certain odors to others. Cernoch and Porter (1985) found that 12–18-day-old breastfeeding children preferred the odor of their mother's sweat – collected on gauze pads from her underarm the night before – to that of another woman. Bottle-feeding children who were not breastfeeding showed no similar preference for their mother's or father's odor. This suggests that children learn to recognize their mother's odor in connection with breastfeeding, while bottle-feeding children are not as close to their mother's underarm and therefore not equally familiar with her odor.

Newborns also show preferences for familiar non-maternal odors, and **gender differences** seem to be present early on. Balogh and Porter (1986) fastened a gauze pad with the odor of cherry or ginger to the inside of newborn infants' bassinets for one day. When they

DOI: 10.4324/9781003292463-6

were tested shortly after, the girls, but not the boys, preferred the familiar odor. This may be because girls are physiologically some-what more mature at birth than boys. The importance of odors is also demonstrated by the fact that children aged 7–15 months spent less time exploring unknown objects, especially with their mouths, when unfamiliar odors had been added to the objects. The unfamiliar odor caused the children to be cautious (Durand et al., 2008).

Although children show an ability to distinguish between important odors early on, older children are far better at recognizing odors than younger children, and adults are better than older children. Through-out childhood, girls exceed boys in their ability to distinguish odors and are also more aware of them (Ferdenzi et al., 2008).

Taste

Taste and nutrition are related. During the first week of life, children develop a complex system to regulate their own food intake. New-borns show a consistent preference for foods with a sweet taste rather than for sour, salty, bitter or tasteless foods (Steiner et al., 2001). They generally respond to sweet-tasting liquids with a relaxed expression reminiscent of a smile and often lick their lips. Sour liquids result in pursed lips and a wrinkled nose. Bitter liquids cause infants to gape open and stick out their tongue as if to squeeze out the bitter taste (Rosenstein & Oster, 1988). The common preference for sweet tastes is easy to change, however. Infants who are allergic to milk are often given a substitute that does not taste as sweet. They get used to it quickly and soon prefer the substitute to regular milk. As the flavor of breast milk varies somewhat depending on the mother's diet, infants become used to different flavors and will accept food more easily if they are already familiar with its taste from their mother's breast milk (Nicklaus, 2009). The **enculturation** of taste thus already begins with breast milk.

Children are born with a set of innate preferences and aversions that dominate at an early age, while new impressions and experiences become more important after the first 3 months (Harris, 1997). During the first 2 years of life, a change takes place from internal to external cues, from congenital and hunger-driven to socially determined pref-erences. Around the age of 2, children's preferences begin to become established. They become more discerning, begin to reject food and eat less varied foods. While only 19 percent of 4–6-month-olds are considered to be picky by their mothers, the number rises to 50 percent at the age of 2 (Carruth et al., 2004; Nicklaus, 2009). However, 2-year-olds who eat different types of food have the most varied diet at the age of 5 (Cox et al., 1997). It is also at the age of 5 that children first begin to show the same dislike of the kinds of foods that are generally disliked by people in their culture (Rozin, 1989). The period in which children eat less varied food lasts until the age of 8, after which they slowly become more willing to try new foods. Studies nevertheless show that a varied diet is important early on, as the differences between 2–3-year-olds can actually be traced all the way into adulthood (Nicklaus et al., 2005).

6

Intermodal Perception

Intermodal perception is the ability to recognize the same "**object**" with more than one sense, such as recognizing something by touch one has previously only seen. This is necessary in order for children to form a comprehensive understanding of the world as well as to establish experiential *constancy* across the senses. They must be able to distinguish between "natural" relationships, such as the connection between the movement and sound of a bouncing ball, and incidental relationships, such as when a dog barks and the phone rings at the same time. The question is how the child comes to relate information from one sense to information from other senses.

Here, too, Gibson and Piaget take opposing views. Gibson's theory (1979) is based on *differentiation*, arguing that the senses initially constitute a primitive unity and gradually become differentiated. At first, all the senses are equal in that they provide information about the qualities of the same object, but directed at different types of energy. It is possible to demonstrate an emerging intermodal organization at birth, such as when children only a few hours after being born turn in the direction of a sound (see Chapter 4, this volume). According to Piaget's (1952) *integration theory*, the senses are initially separate and become integrated through a child's actions and the experience of simultaneous impressions from several senses. His view is supported by the finding that 6-month-olds showed visual recognition of objects they had seen before, but not of similar objects they had only explored by touch (Rose & Ruff, 1987).

Gottlieb and associates (2006) argue that both theories are too simple. They point to the fact that the senses do not develop simultaneously – either during fetal development or later – and

DOI: 10.4324/9781003292463-7

therefore cannot derive from a single sense as suggested by Gibson. By the time a child is born, the auditory sense has already begun to develop, while their visual sense is first put to functional use after birth. Although partly agreeing with Piaget, they add that intermodal perception is not a uniform process but a result of interaction between the senses in different situations and for different purposes. The temporal differences in development may be of importance to the processing of sensory stimulation. Moreover, the senses are specialized for different types of sensory input from the outset. The auditory system, for example, is specialized to process sequentially organized stimulation, while the visual system is best at spatial perception. Visual and auditory perception are thus characterized by altogether different properties, and either one of the two senses will be more prominent depending on the context (Lewkowicz, 1994).

Studies of children's reactions to *amodal information* contribute to an understanding of the development of intermodal integration, information that does not derive from a single **sensory modality**, but from across two or more senses such as time, space, rhythm and intensity. The movements and sounds of a speaking mouth or a bouncing ball are completely synchronous. Bahrick and Lickliter (2000, 2014) agree with Gibson that integration is inherent in the senses. The perceptual system is constructed in such a way that amodal information recruits attention, and young infants are more attentive to amodal information than to information from only a single sense. In one study, 4-month-olds were shown two superimposed videos of two pairs of clapping hands. When adults look at such double images of two hands clapping without sound, they perceive both pairs of hands as ambiguous and vague. When they hear the sound of one pair of hands, they perceive the movement of that pair more clearly, while the movement of the second pair fades into the background. After the superimposed video without sound had been shown to children, they looked equally long at both pairs of hands when these were shown simultaneously, but with each pair on its own screen. After the children had heard the sound of one pair of hands clapping on the superimposed video, they looked longer at the screen with the other pair of hands. **Preference for novelty** is typical for this age (see Book 1, *Theoretical Perspectives and Methodology*, Chapter 25). The results therefore suggest that the pair of hands with sound visually stood out for the children as well, just as it does for adults. The clapping hands without synchronous sound receded into the background and received less attention and were thus perceived as novel when shown by themselves on a screen (Bahrick et al., 1981).

According to Bahrick (2004), amodal experiences form a basis for the development of intermodal perception and an understanding of the relationships between different aspects of the complex sensory environment. When stimulation is not amodal, infants focus on a single sense, thereby promoting the development of detailed perception within that particular sense. Unimodal and amodal experiences thus complement each other during development. Toward the end of the first year, children become better at regulating their own perceptual exploration of the environment. Adults, too, are sensitive to the synchronicity of amodal perceptual stimulation and may experience discomfort when dubbing or poor synchronization results in mouth movements that are out of synch with the sounds of speech in a movie.

Hearing or vision impairments will influence intermodal perception, but it is not known how this may impact other sensory modalities and the development of perception in general.

Summary of Part I

1   The senses are functional at birth, but not fully developed. It takes time for a child to use its senses in the same way as an adult. Children get better at perceiving what is common in their environment and worse at perceiving things that occur only rarely. The visual and auditory systems have characteristics that promote children's social orientation.

2   According to Piaget, perception occurs "indirectly" – children construct their perception by interacting with objects (in the broadest sense). Gibson's ecological theory maintains that infants' perceptual equipment "fits" the environment and thus allows them to perceive "directly" without learning. Children automatically perceive possibilities for action or *affordances*. Perception leads to action, the opposite of Piaget's view. There is research to support both views, and a number of theorists believe that the development of perception includes elements of both theories. According to Bremner, the most important milestone in perceptual development is children's ability to use their perceptual knowledge to guide their own actions.

3   Most aspects of visual perception show a rapid development during the first year. There is disagreement about the importance of innate abilities and experience for this development. Normal development of vision is dependent on relevant visual experiences.

4   Right after birth, infants "prefer" the visual features typical of faces. According to Carey, children have an innate module for facial recognition, while Slater and Butterworth maintain that early facial recognition is an expression of children's overall aptitude for learning. With increasing age, children improve at

distinguishing faces in their own environment, while their ability to recognize faces of people from races of which they have less experience declines.

5   Children get better at integrating multiple visual elements and gradually become more susceptible to optical illusions. Throughout infancy, children improve at using representations of reality in images and videos as a "map" and begin to understand when a photo or a video depicts themselves.

6   Visual impairment affects all areas of development, particularly orientation and mobility. Children with visual impairments often have a delayed motor development and can be passive. They use sound to orient themselves physically, emotionally and socially. Blind children engage in joint attention, and language is often one of their strengths. Because of their unique experience, they use words in a somewhat different way. Many children with severe visual impairment have multiple disorders.

7   Newborns are able to distinguish between all aspects of auditory stimulation, but have higher hearing thresholds than older children and adults and require varied acoustic stimulation to develop full auditory perception. Early auditory attention is directed at human voices.

8   Newborns can *localize* sound approximately and are able to locate sounds with increasing accuracy in the course of the first 2 years of life. At the end of the first year, visual and auditory localization are fairly well integrated.

9   Hearing impairments affect children's orientation in the environment and their speech. Communication and speech can be supported by improving the perception of sound and facilitating visual communication. Many children with a severe hearing impairment benefit from a cochlear implant, but need additional visual support. Some function best using sign language. Many children with hearing impairments also have other disorders such as **ADHD** and **learning disorders**. Children with hearing impairments are socially vulnerable and have a higher rate of behavioral and emotional problems than others.

10 Children show an early interest in music. They are able to recognize short melodies and tonal patterns and make up "babbling songs." Musical ability has a certain genetic basis, but musicality also requires an environment that fosters the development of such

skills. Musical preferences emerge gradually and reflect the child's experiences and culture.

11 The development of *smell* and *taste* is largely controlled by innate preferences and aversions at an early age, while new impressions and experiences gradually become more important. Later eating habits can be traced back to a varied diet during early childhood.

12 According to Gibson's *differentiation theory*, the senses initially constitute a primitive unity and gradually become differentiated, whereas Piaget's *integration theory* maintains that the senses are separate at first and gradually become integrated. Gottlieb and colleagues propose that the development of *intermodal perception* is a *dynamic process* that incorporates both differentiation and integration. *Amodal information* can be experienced with several senses at the same time. It assumes attentional precedence during early perception and lays the foundation for a child's understanding of what belongs together and to establish context.

Core Issues

- The role of action in the development of perception.
- Developmental differentiation or integration of the senses.

Suggestions for Further Reading

Bahrick, L. E., Walker, A. S., & Neisser, U. (1981). Selective looking by infants. *Cognitive Psychology, 13,* 377–390.

Fantz, R. L. (1961). The origin of form perception. *Scientific American, 204,* 66–72.

Fraiberg, S. (1977). *Insights from the blind.* New York, NY: Basic Books.

Leibold, L. J. (2012). Development of auditory scene analysis and auditory attention. In L. A. Werner, A. N. Popper, & R. R. Fay (Eds), *Human auditory development* (pp. 137–161). New York, NY: Springer.

Part II

Motor Development

7
Motor Functions

Physical actions are movements with an intention and a goal. Motor development is an adaptive process that allows children to gradually overcome gravitational forces, to plan, coordinate, perform and evaluate actions, and to create new physical and social opportunities for action. Action forms the basis for developing cooperative skills as well as **autonomy**. During the first years of life, children go through significant motor development that leads to important changes in how they explore and relate to their physical and social surroundings.

Compared with many newborn animals, the motor skills of human children are extremely limited at birth. The most important early skills are a rudimentary head control and the ability to suckle when nourishment is offered, but infants make increasing use of the actions required by different situations and the opportunities they provide. Action control, however, is not confined to the brain alone. Movements are performed by the body, and physical growth implies a continuous adaptation of these movements to a body that grows in size and changes in proportion.

Action means planning. Actions must be adapted to the properties of things and expected movements, or *prospective control*. When children catch a ball, they must assess its size in order to gauge the correct distance between their hands and anticipate the ball's movement. Unless the movement is "planned" and has been initiated before the ball arrives, the child's hands will react too late. Therefore, the development of motor skills is largely a matter of coordinating perception and movement (Adolph & Robinson, 2015; von Hofsten, 2007). Although severely impaired vision affects a child's motor development (see Chapter 3, this volume), it is not dependent on the child's ability to see, but on some way of perceiving the environment.

DOI: 10.4324/9781003292463-9

Motor development affects children's functioning in many ways. Their ability for independent locomotion increases their room for action and entails psychological reorganization (Anderson et al., 2014; Campos et al., 2000). It allows children access to new experiences and activities, to explore people, things and events more independently and to investigate the properties of objects. Children can take a more active role in play and interaction and approach caregivers, other children and adults they may be interested in on their own. They become more aware of people and things that are farther removed from them and develop a greater need for emotional information about what may be dangerous and what may be positive, about what to stay away from and what they might explore. They look more toward their mother when she moves away and begin to seek out emotional information from her and from others (social referencing; see Book 6, *Emotions, Temperament, Personality, Moral, Prosocial and Antisocial Development,* Chapter 6). Greater mobility means greater freedom, but also more constraints. Adults must be more attentive to children's whereabouts and guide as well as limit their exploration.

Children's development of motor skills also affects the *transactional* processes. When a child acquires new motor skills and a larger repertoire of actions, parents gain more insight into their child's perception, thoughts and feelings about the world and surrounding

Joe Campos

activities and the child's interests and intentions. This affects parents' reactions, expectations and demands of their child, which in turn affect the child's actions and so on (see Book 1, *Theoretical Perspectives and Methodology,* Chapter 6). Parents experience that their child's increasingly independent mobility changes the family's interaction patterns, owing to both the need for increased monitoring and limitation of the child's actions and the child's development of independence, self-reliance and autonomy (Biringen et al., 2008; Campos et al., 2000).

8

From Action Systems to Complex Actions

Some of children' earliest movements are **developmental reflexes** that only occur during infancy. They are the result of evolutionary processes and provide early action tendencies that have been and continue to be important for a child's survival (Table 8.1). A touch on the lips, for example, induces a newborn to suck. Once the **rooting reflex** has helped a child find its mother's nipple (see the following), the *sucking reflex* initiates the intake of food. A child's early repertoire of actions contributes to nourishment and survival, but also initiates the development of movement and provides children with experience of the environment (von Hofsten, 2007).

Some developmental reflexes are activated by internal and external factors. The rooting reflex for example causes the infant to turn his head toward the side being stimulated. It is usually elicited when the infant is stroked across the cheek, but not when he does so himself or when he is not hungry. Placing the infant's cheek near the mother's breast will help him find the nipple, while trying to push the infant's opposite cheek to get his mouth in the right place is counterproductive, as he will search for the nipple on the side being touched. This illustrates how developmental reflexes lead to self-initiated actions rather than actions imposed on the infant by others. Nor is the infant's suckling action automatic, but adapted to the amount of milk. Infants do not begin to suckle reflexively once they are satiated, even if their lips are stimulated.

Developmental reflexes are thus not entirely reflexive, but rather form a set of *action systems* that are activated under certain external conditions. They gradually lose their reflexive character to be replaced by more deliberately controlled actions. Children continue to suck after the sucking reflex has disappeared; the difference is that the

DOI: 10.4324/9781003292463-10

Table 8.1 Some developmental reflexes (based on Gallahue & Ozmun, 2006)

Babinski reflex	The child's big toe flexes upwards and the other toes fan out when a sharp object is stroked backwards along the lateral side of the foot. Usually begins to disappear at 3 months of age
Palmar grasp reflex	The fingers close when the child's palm is lightly touched. Usually disappears at 2–4 months of age
Moro reflex	The child stretches out her arms and moves them toward the body's midline when the head suddenly loses support. Usually disappears at 5–6 months of age
Plantar reflex	Replaces the Babinski reflex around the age of 4 months. The toes flex down when the ball of the foot is stimulated. Usually disappears at 9–10 months of age
Rooting reflex	The child turns her head toward the side being stimulated when lightly touched on the cheek. Most pronounced at 3 weeks of age; gradually subsides and disappears at around 11 months of age
Sucking reflex	Stimulation of the lips and the mouth elicits a sucking action. Present at birth, disappears at around 3 months of age
Asymmetric tonic neck reflex	When the child herself or someone else turns the child's head to one side, the arm and the leg on that side will extend. Usually disappears at around 6 months of age

sucking is not as easily activated by external factors alone. Similarly, newborns can only grip with their hand when something touches their palm. Only a few months later, infants will reach for objects and adapt their grip to the object's size and will not try to reach for objects that clearly are too far away (von Hofsten, 2007). These early action tendencies are important because they help children develop exploratory movements and learn. Their disappearance, or the loss of their reflexive character, is nonetheless a significant developmental milestone, and children's learning gains momentum around the age of 3 months, coinciding with their growing social awareness.

Children's earliest engagement in activities typically involves the whole body. An interesting event causes a child to watch actively, but also to move her mouth, tongue and arms (Smitsman, 2001). An important part of development is for children to learn to confine themselves to movements that are relevant to the situation to be explored and the actions to be taken.

Children's early repertoire of developmental reflexes and action systems forms the basis for developing a broad and varied repertoire of actions. The transition from simple to more complex actions is often characterized by a reduced level of efficiency. Children are able to move much faster by crawling for example than by walking when taking their first steps. Although children do occasionally crawl during this phase when they want to get somewhere quickly, they will mostly try to move on two legs, even if it means that they fall. This illustrates the importance of independent action and the intrinsic motivation provided by physical mastery, and perhaps also by moving just like older children and adults. In addition, it is faster to walk across longer distances, and walking increases the child's range and makes it easier to carry things. There are thus many advantages to walking versus crawling (Adolph & Tamis-LeMonda, 2014).

9

Gross Motor Development

Gross motor skills include control of the body's posture, crawling, walking and other forms of locomotion.

Early Development

During early gross motor development, children gradually overcome the forces of gravity. Some early milestones are shown in Figure 9.1. Newborns are able to turn their head from one side to the other when lying on their stomach, for example to orient themselves to a sound. At 3 months, children are usually able to hold their head up and look straight ahead. They support themselves by leaning on their forearms and are able to turn their face to both sides. The ability to maintain an upright head position is important for children to visually explore the surroundings. It also makes it easier for parents and others to discover the child's interests and further encourage these through interaction. Early motor development thus affects the interaction between children and parents (Prechtl, 1993).

Usually, children are able to turn from side to back when they are about 2 months old. A little later, they can sit with the support of their arms, and about half of all 6–7-month- olds can sit without supporting themselves. At 9 months, they are able to move from a lying to a sitting position, and, at 11 months, most infants can stand on their own.

The first independent locomotion usually occurs by rolling at the age of 5–6 months of age. At 10 months, children can walk with help and support, and a little later by themselves. This changes the perception of the surroundings as children look down when they crawl and ahead when they walk (Kretch et al., 2014). At 2 years of age, children begin to climb stairs. However, the acquisition of these and other

DOI: 10.4324/9781003292463-11

——————— 50 percent

- - - - - - - - - 90 percent

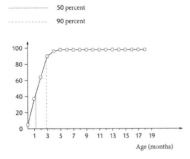

Lifting the head. The child raises her head 45 degrees at the midline and maintains the position for a limited time. Weight is on the hands, forearms and chest.

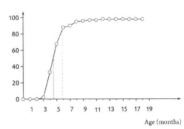

Hands to feet. The child lifts her feet and raises them so that her hand touches one or both feet. The child can hold her legs in the middle of the body.

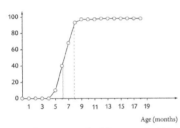

Sitting without arm support. The child can sit comfortably for longer periods with the weight on her bottom/legs without falling. The arms are extended, and the child can play with a toy.

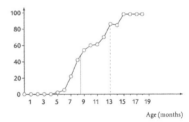

Crawling (early pattern). The weight is on the opposite hand and knee, shifting from one side to the other.

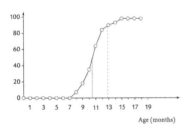

Standing without support. The child quickly finds her balance and stands on her own with the weight on her feet.

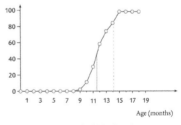

Walking without support. The child walks without support, but the walking pattern is still immature.

Figure 9.1 Selected gross motor skills and their development.

The curves indicate the percentage of children who master a given skill at different ages. Age levels at which 50 and 90 percent of all children master a skill are highlighted (after Piper & Darrah, 1994, pp. 84, 130, 162 and 171).

skills shows significant variation in age (see Figure 9.1). The specified ages should therefore be understood to be typical ages, and somewhat earlier or later acquisition of skills generally does not indicate an abnormal development. Additionally, there is considerable variation in how children solve the challenge of independent locomotion. They scoot, roll, jump, kick and crawl forward using their arms, legs, chest, elbows, stomach and back. Children also use different strategies when they learn to walk: some use a "stepping" strategy, others twist their body back and forth, some move sideways while holding onto furniture or initiate movement by letting their body "fall" forward (Snapp-Childs & Corbetta, 2009). The reasons for this variation are unknown. Some of them probably reflect children's active exploration of possible actions in their physical surroundings; others seem to be the result of sheer coincidence, lack of mastery or "sensory-motor noise." Thus, variation represents an important developmental element here as well. Each child chooses the strategies that work best (Adolph & Robinson, 2015). Blind children move less to explore, and their motor skills develop later owing to a lack of visual incentives for exploration and movement (Freedman & Cannady, 1971).

Further Gross Motor Development

Motor development continues after the child has passed the first milestones and learned to walk. Most children learn to run, jump and hop, and to walk on various surfaces as well as uphill and downhill. At 18 months, children begin to run and improve until the age of 2–3 years, but running first becomes effective at the age of 4–5. Children are generally about 3 years old before they can hop three times on one foot. Around the age of 5, they can jump a distance of about 1 meter and 30 centimeters in height. Until the age of 12, boys jump only a little farther than girls, but from here on the differences become increasingly pronounced. More culture-bound motor skills such as riding a bike, playing soccer or swimming continue to evolve throughout school age, and even longer for those who pursue them as a sport. Development is about more than simply mastering or not mastering a skill – the *qualitative* execution of many established motor skills improves throughout childhood and adolescence (Largo et al., 2001a, b).

10

Development of Fine Motor Skills

Fine motor skills include all the movements of the hands, such as pointing, gripping and drawing. Fine motor skills make it possible for children to manually handle and explore things.

Early Development

Early development is above all characterized by the ability to grip and hold with increasing precision and to adjust the grip of the hand to objects of various shapes and sizes (Figure 10.1). Even a fetus brings its hand to its mouth, and the coordination of this movement increases rapidly during the first 6 months of life. If an object is placed in the hand of a child at this age, they will usually move it to their mouth. It is not necessary for them to see the object first, as they perform just as well in darkness.

The ability to let go develops later; children are unable to let go of objects until they are about 4 months old. At this age, children also begin to look at the object they hold in their hand before moving it to their mouth. As the child's grip improves, the movement of the hand adjusts to the object about to be grasped, and, at the end of the first year, the shape of the hand anticipates the object's size, an ability that requires visual control. At 9 months, children begin to use the **pincer grip**, which enables them to pick up very small objects (Bertenthal & Clifton, 1998; Rochat, 1993).

A parallel development takes place in children's hand movements toward objects. To begin with, the movements are brief and imprecise and depend on suitable physical conditions. The hand rarely reaches its goal. Furthermore, newborns automatically open their hand when extending it and thus fail to close it around objects that are further

DOI: 10.4324/9781003292463-12

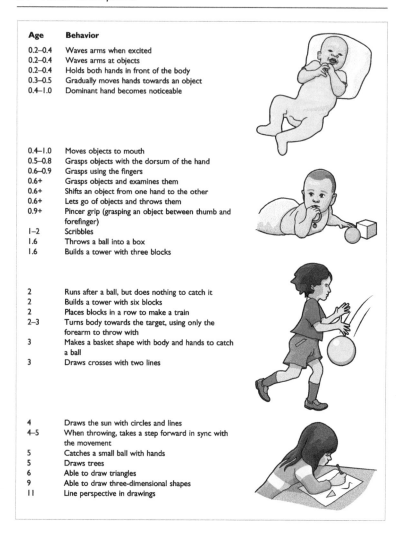

Age	Behavior
0.2–0.4	Waves arms when excited
0.2–0.4	Waves arms at objects
0.2–0.4	Holds both hands in front of the body
0.3–0.5	Gradually moves hands towards an object
0.4–1.0	Dominant hand becomes noticeable
0.4–1.0	Moves objects to mouth
0.5–0.8	Grasps objects with the dorsum of the hand
0.6–0.9	Grasps using the fingers
0.6+	Grasps objects and examines them
0.6+	Shifts an object from one hand to the other
0.6+	Lets go of objects and throws them
0.9+	Pincer grip (grasping an object between thumb and forefinger)
1–2	Scribbles
1.6	Throws a ball into a box
1.6	Builds a tower with three blocks
2	Runs after a ball, but does nothing to catch it
2	Builds a tower with six blocks
2	Places blocks in a row to make a train
2–3	Turns body towards the target, using only the forearm to throw with
3	Makes a basket shape with body and hands to catch a ball
3	Draws crosses with two lines
4	Draws the sun with circles and lines
4–5	When throwing, takes a step forward in sync with the movement
5	Catches a small ball with hands
5	Draws trees
6	Able to draw triangles
9	Able to draw three-dimensional shapes
11	Line perspective in drawings

Figure 10.1 Some milestones in the development of fine motor skills.

Children begin to use their hands for many different purposes early on. Age indicates when the action is observed in the majority of children.

away. At 2 months, infants will generally clench their hand when reaching for something, while at the same time extending less frequently than before. When manual extension once again increases in frequency 1½ months later, their hand is open, and at 4–5 months of age they begin to succeed when reaching out to grasp an item. The ability to grasp moving objects requires forward control and coordination of information about the object's path and the infant's own movements. Nevertheless, infants begin to anticipate and reach for the location of moving objects at around the same time as they begin to grasp stationary items (von Hofsten, 2004, 2007).

The fact that infants begin to reach for things is also important for the interaction with other children and adults. Exactly what they reach for provides the most important clue to what infants are interested in.

Further Development of Fine Motor Skills

Around the age of 2–3 years, children develop the ability to throw and catch a ball, but around the age of 6 they are able to perform these skills in a more competent way (Gallahue & Ozmun, 2006).

At the end of their first year of life, children begin to use tools to extend their reach, such as a small rake to get hold of something they cannot reach with their hands. Other tools at this age are usually used for eating, drinking and drawing. Learning to eat with a spoon illustrates this gradual process. Toward the end of the first year, children begin to use a spoon in different ways: putting it on a plate, pounding it on the table, switching it from hand to hand and occasionally putting it in their mouth. A little later they try to eat with it but, even if they are able to hold the spoon, they find it difficult to fill it with food and move it to their mouth. The spoon does not become an independent eating utensil until they approach the age of 2 years. Chinese children master the necessary motor skills for chopstick use at 4½ years but need 2 more years before they can eat half of their meal independently (Wong et al., 2002).

Toward the end of the second year, children also begin to use pencils and crayons. Until the age of 3–4 years, most children use a fist grip to hold a pencil. This grip develops until children are taught to use an "adult" writing grip in kindergarten or school. Writing is a complex process, and children's handwriting progressively becomes faster, more coherent and more automatized in the course of the first years of school, in line with their general motor development. A 12-year-old writes about 50 percent faster than a 9-year-old. Girls' handwriting is generally somewhat "neater" than that of boys (Connolly & Dalgleish, 1993; Søvik, 1993).

Fine and Gross Motor Skills Are Related

The development of fine and gross motor skills is part of the same process, and the distinction between them is more a matter of convenience than fact. Body control is necessary for children to be able to perform independent actions with their arms and hands, and the loss of balance when reaching for an interesting object will lead the child to find sturdy ways of sitting and moving. An important development thus takes place when children handle objects as a result of changes in gross motor skills, which in turn are motivated by the desire to perform fine motor actions. Being able to sit for longer periods without support is a prerequisite for children's ability to reach for objects without tumbling over. Children who are not yet able to sit upright without help reach for objects with both hands when they are supported, while children who can sit on their own reach for objects with one hand. The same applies to the development of independent locomotion: once children begin to slide forward on their belly and start to crawl, objects lying beyond reach provide an incentive for locomotion. Children who can walk on their own carry things in a different way than children who crawl or who have to support themselves (Adolph & Robinson, 2015; Goldfield & Wolff, 2004).

Children's early movements are frequently exploratory and often performed with a high degree of self-control, demanding considerable attention and cognitive resources. Gradually, their movements become *automatized*. This is a prerequisite for the fluid performance of motor skills and also reduces the amount of cognitive resources involved in performing movements. A well-acquired skill thus requires fewer resources. Children with motor difficulties need to use more cognitive resources to perform movements and are thus left with fewer resources for actual play and the solving of "tasks."

DOI: 10.4324/9781003292463-13

Individual and Cultural Differences

Children show significant differences with regard to when they master various skills, as well as the quality of execution (Adolph & Robinson, 2015). Although some of these differences are due to biological factors, experience is important as well. This becomes evident when comparing cultures with different routines of childcare. In some African cultures, mothers believe it is necessary to teach their children to overcome gravity and train them in motor skills such as sitting and standing. They develop these skills earlier than North American children, whose mothers do not instruct their children in a similar way, but they do not show a correspondingly early development in other motor skills (Konner, 1976; Super, 1981). Similarly, environments that do not promote children's independent locomotion may delay the development of children's ability to walk. Children who are swaddled much of the day – wrapped tightly in cloth or a similar material – have a delayed motor development. Chinese children who spend much of their time in a bed with fluffy pillows that are difficult to walk on generally begin to walk about 3 months later than children in the US (Adolph & Robinson, 2015; Campos et al., 2000).

Many motor skills develop in a more or less fixed order, but there is always some variation. Most children crawl before they begin to walk, but some of them follow other **developmental paths**. Some children move by pushing themselves forward on their buttocks and start to walk without ever having crawled (Hopkins et al., 1993). It has been argued that children who do not crawl or otherwise deviate from the **typical sequence of development** may have difficulty reading and writing at school because of this (Holle, 1981), but this is not supported by research (White et al., 2006). Some children will indeed have difficulty learning to read and write, both among those

DOI: 10.4324/9781003292463-14

who crawl and those who do not crawl. Therefore, absence of crawling is neither a defect nor a sign of abnormal development, but an expression of the fact that children follow different developmental paths toward the same goal (Largo et al., 1985). It is the biological foundation, together with the childcare routines (for example how the child is usually placed), that determines a child's path of development (Hopkins & Butterworth, 1997; Iverson, 2010).

13

Theories of Motor Development

Maturation has traditionally been emphasized in motor development, but recent theories give experience a greater role.

Maturation

For a long time, motor development was generally seen as the result of neurological maturation based on a genetically determined time-table, while experience was considered to be of limited importance (Schmuckler, 2013). New movements were believed to originate as a result of the brain's formation of nerve structures that control the performance of these movements (see McGraw, 1943). In a classic experiment, one of two identical female twins was trained to walk a staircase 10 minutes every day for 6 weeks, between the ages of 46 and 52 weeks. At the end of this period, it took her 26 seconds to walk the stairs. The other twin, who had not received training, began to climb stairs by herself when she was 49 weeks old and was able to walk the training stairs in 45 seconds 4 weeks later. At this point, she received the equivalent training her sister had been given, 10 minutes a day for 2 weeks. After that, she could walk the stairs in 10 seconds, faster than her sister, with far longer experience, was able to do (Gesell & Thompson, 1929). Experience thus played a role, but Gesell interpreted the result to indicate that, although training does have an effect, it is of limited value before neurological maturation has progressed far enough.

Dynamic Models

From the perspective of dynamic models, children's movements develop as part of a **self-organizing** system that consists of many internal and external processes and sub-processes (see Book 1,

DOI: 10.4324/9781003292463-15

Theoretical Perspectives and Methodology, Chapter 7). Although general neurological development is of importance, it is only one of several interacting processes. Every movement involves a number of conditions: adequate neurological maturation, related motor functions, muscle strength, experience and the physical environment. The underlying processes originate at different times and develop at somewhat different paces. Only once the necessary processes are functional are children able to develop new movements, which in turn are adapted to constantly new objects and environments. All motor activity is dependent on a complex hierarchy of support structures in the form of body posture and affordances in the environment. Their organization varies depending on the action chosen by a child and whether the child is in a lying, sitting or standing position (Adolph & Robinson, 2015).

Thelen and Smith (1994) use a **dynamic systems** approach to explain the emergence of walking. In their view, walking is the result of an infant's intention to move toward something, its neurological and perceptual development and physical prerequisites, such as sufficient leg muscle strength to support the body as well as move the legs. In addition, environmental conditions must allow for the possibility of walking, for example something the child can hang on to while still unable to walk steadily, or an adult who supports some of the weight while the child's muscle power still lacks the necessary strength. If any of these conditions are not sufficiently met, the child will not walk.

Newborns perform walking movements with their legs when they are held upright and a light pressure is applied to the bottom of their feet. Although these movements disappear after about 2 months and do not return until the child learns to walk a few months later, Thelen and Smith believe that their neurological basis is maintained, but that the movements are suppressed because children must first develop sufficient muscle strength and body control to overcome gravity. To support their view, they point out that a 3-month-old placed upright in water that provides buoyancy will perform the same walking movements with the feet as a newborn. Other scientists argue that these early walking movements have not been "preserved" as Thelen and Smith claim, but that they have an altogether different neurological basis precisely because the legs have the power to carry the body under normal gravitational conditions (Adolph & Robinson, 2015).

Primary Movement Patterns, Variation and Selection

The theory of **neuronal group selection** is based on the assumption that a structure of primary neuron groups (nerve cell connections) responsible for motor functions has formed in the course of evolution, and that this structure changes as the result of experience based on variation, exploration and selection of movements (Edelman, 1989). A genetically determined starting repertoire of general movement patterns emerges at different age levels. These patterns are further selected through experience and adapted to the environment. The *phase of primary variability* begins early in fetal development and continues throughout the first few months after birth. The infant tries out different movements and chooses the most appropriate among them. Yet these early movements entail only a rough adaptation to the environment. They are followed by the *phases of selection*, involving different age levels for various skills such as grasping, crawling and walking. Each selection phase is followed by a *phase of secondary variability* in which variation in movement leads to a more specific adaptation to different environments (Hadders-Algra, 2002).

In contrast to dynamic models, Edelman's theory places more emphasis on maturation owing to the assumption of a basic set of innate movement patterns. It differs from other theories of maturation in that maturation alone does not bring about the infant's final movements, but only general movement patterns that must be further developed through experience (Piek, 2002).

14

Development of Drawing

In many cultures, children begin to use pencils and crayons early – during their second year of life – but drawing takes time to learn. The earliest drawings mostly consist of scribbles that gradually become more distinct and detailed. Barely half of the drawings of human figures made by 4-year-olds include the feet and arms; at 6 years of age, over 90 percent of the drawings include the feet. About 70 percent of all 6-year-olds and 90 percent of 10-year-olds draw the arms. Very few 4-year-olds draw the neck and hair. Only at the age of 8 do half of all children include the neck. A similar percentage include the hair a year later (Aronsson, 1997).

The development of drawing skills reflects general motor development, changes in the ability to perceive and abstract characteristics of people and things in the environment and the development of interests and creativity. Children's drawings reflect both their perception of reality and the particular aspects of the environment that capture their attention. At 3 years of age, children are able to explain what their drawings represent when asked about them. Before this age, it is not always easy to recognize realistic elements in their drawings. However, scribbling does not merely produce scribbles: it represents mom, a house, a cat and so on. Scribbling also has its own aesthetic and reflects the way in which a child tries to represent a three-dimensional world on a two-dimensional sheet of paper (Arnheim, 1974). When children create a graphical representation, they choose certain aspects of the object they want to draw (Aronsson, 1997). When asked to depict a potato field, a 7-year-old drew potatoes that were visible through the soil (Figure 14.1). The main characteristic of a potato field is, after all, potatoes, which is why they had to be visible.

DOI: 10.4324/9781003292463-16

Painting is a popular child activity in many cultures

Children's drawings are influenced by the environment they live in, including general cultural influences as well as the culture's particular drawing traditions. In industrialized countries, young children spend a lot of time drawing, and with increasing age their drawings gradually become more culturally conventional (Winner, 2006). Training and drawing traditions are of major importance. A survey conducted in a remote region of Papua New Guinea, an area with no tradition of graphic art, found major differences between human figure drawings made by children who had gone to school and received drawing instruction and those by children who had not attended school (Martlew & Connolly, 1996). The children who attended school drew conventional drawings, while many of those who were unschooled produced scribbles and shapes. A few children drew relatively advanced human figures. The study demonstrates the importance of training and experience for developing drawing skills. Drawing is not merely a matter of learning how to use a pencil; the general graphic culture is of significance as well. Studies of children's drawings show the important

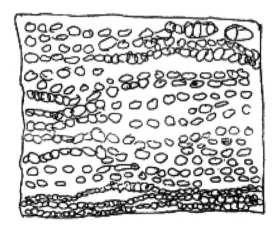

Figure 14.1 Potato field.

Children often draw elements that are important for the picture's theme, although not visible in reality. In this picture, a 7-year-old depicting a potato field drew potatoes that can be seen through the soil (from Luquet, 1927).

influence of the kinds of drawings children are exposed to, such as comic strips (Wilson & Wilson, 1977).

There are considerable individual differences in drawing skills and artistic ability. Edvard Munch and many other famous painters showed signs of talent early on. Some children with **Down syndrome**, autism spectrum disorders and other forms of **atypical development** also show exceptional drawing skills (Mullin, 2014; Xia, 2014).

15

Atypical Motor Development

Motor disorders impact children's independent mobility and use of hands, as well as their participation in many common activities. Gross motor skills are of particular importance for exploring surroundings, participating socially and feeling secure. Fine motor skills are used for exploring things in the environment, handling objects, building and constructing, using eating utensils, drawing and other things and thus are important for a child's ability to independently participate in meals, play and other activities. For children with motor impairment, many ordinary skills are more difficult to acquire and have a delayed development. They take more cognitive resources, and, when fewer resources are available for other purposes, such as paying attention to what happens in one's surroundings while performing an action, it can impact children's understanding of social relationships and the development of language and social skills. Motor training may be necessary at the expense of other activities. For children with more severe disabilities, this can involve considerable amounts of time.

Children with motor impairments have a higher incidence of many types of disorders, with major variations in cognitive and **language functioning** (Odding et al., 2006; Stadskleiv et al., 2017). Symptoms of attentional problems are common among children with **cerebral palsy** (Bjørgaas et al., 2012). Some of them have learning disorders, including problems with mathematics and learning how to read and write (Dahlgren Sandberg, 2006). Also, boys with Duchenne muscular dystrophy have difficulty reading and writing (Banihani et al., 2015). Children with more severe motor impairments have a greater number of cognitive disorders – especially **intellectual disability** – than children with more moderate motor impairments, but there is no direct relationship between motor impairment and general cognitive functioning. While

DOI: 10.4324/9781003292463-17

studies have found that 60 percent of all children with cerebral palsy and impairment in both arms and legs score below 70 on intelligence tests, the results indicate that 40 percent scored within or above the normal range (Andersen et al., 2008; Sigurdardottir et al., 2008). Thus, motor functioning does not provide a basis for drawing conclusions about the individual child's cognitive functions (Blair, 2010). The disorders may have a neurological basis, but, like all other development, disorders are the result of interaction between biology and experience (see Book 1, *Theoretical Perspectives and Methodology*, Chapter 7). Theories of cognitive development and **self-regulation** place emphasis on children's actions. Distinguishing between what is directly attributable to a brain injury and what is related to changes in motor experiences is not always possible. There may be cognitive cascade effects from individual motor experiences with fewer possibilities for action, less **automatization** and increased use of cognitive resources to the execution of the earliest actions in infancy. It is commonly observed that children "grow into" their **disability**, and that the differences between them and their peers increase with age.

Minor motor impairments usually have less influence on children's development. They are generally able to perform the same actions as others, but have to use more resources in connection with locomotion, handling objects, drawing and the like. Many children with intellectual disability are clumsy and have coordination problems beyond what one would expect from their intellectual disability.

Children with moderate motor impairments can participate in most activities but need to be more selective in their choice of activities and acquire less experience in many areas. The need to use additional cognitive resources in the performance of activities means that they have less time and get tired more quickly. Often they are less active and function more as observers than participants. They can be left out in some social settings and lose part of the common social life, especially in the phases when children tend to be physically active.

More severe motor disorders impact all areas of the developmental process and affect the child's cognition, language, social interaction and emotional life. Children with severe gross motor impairments participate less actively in play, exploration of the environment and other interactions and find it more difficult to establish contact with other children and adults they may be interested in. The impairment can place major demands on planning and other **executive functions** (see Book 4, *Cognition, Intelligence and Learning*, Chapter 11) and prevent the child from participating in activities that promote these functions (Stadskleiv et al., 2014). Some of these problems can be prevented through early intervention and by adopting measures that afford similar experiences in other ways. A walker or a wheelchair provides better opportunities for exploring the environment and can help children extend their psychological space and autonomy, just as other children experience once they develop independent mobility (Gudgeon & Kirk, 2015). Children with cerebral palsy whose speech is impeded or unintelligible can use communication aids (see Book 5, *Communication and Language Development*, Chapter 11). Despite being unable to speak, language can be their strongest asset, also in connection with play, and they can instruct others to perform play actions they themselves are unable to participate in – language for action.

The developmental consequences of motor impairment thus reach far beyond the motor execution of various actions alone. Even moderate gross and fine motor problems can affect the interaction with parents, siblings and other children and adults, and the child's emotional development, relationships and **personality**. A child's inability to explore and regulate the distance to her parents may affect the

The wheelchair gives children with motor impairment access to mobility and sports

bonding process (see Book 7, *Social Relations, Self-awareness and Identity*, Chapter 4). The need for help has an impact on the development of **self–image** and autonomy. The constant presence of a parent or other adult affects the child's relations with its peers. Children who use a wheelchair state that they feel less disabled when helped by a peer than by an adult (Madge & Fassam, 1982). For children with severe motor impairments, the environment needs to be adapted and must include training for parents and siblings.

Parents of children with cerebral palsy report more emotional and behavioral problems among their children than parents of children without motor disorders (Brossard-Racine et al., 2012). This may reflect the children's frustration with not being able to cope, training fatigue, problems with self-regulation and a difficult social situation with few supportive resources.

Summary of Part II

1   Newborns have a limited repertoire of *reflex actions* that are acti-
    vated under certain external conditions. They are essential for
    survival and help initiate movements that allow children to expe-
    rience the environment. The coordination of perception and
    movement is important in the development of an action reper-
    toire, and motor precision requires *forward control.*

2   *Gross motor skills* overcome the forces of gravity and control body
    posture, crawling, walking and other forms of locomotion. The
    ability to move independently alters the psychological environment
    and affects areas such as **attachment**, language, self-perception
    and autonomy.

3   The development of *fine motor skills* includes all use of the hands
    such as grasping, exploring, handling objects and using *tools*,
    including pencils for drawing and writing. With increasing age,
    many movements become *automatized.*

4   The development of motor skills follows a relatively stable pat-
    tern, with individual variation in relation to how and when skills
    develop. These differences are the result of both biological factors
    and different cultural practices.

5   Traditional explanations of motor development have been based
    on *maturation. Dynamic systems theories* view motor development as
    the result of interaction between the child's individual traits and
    the physical environment. According to the theory of *neuronal
    group selection*, motor development is the result of an evolutionary-
    based set of actions and variation, exploration and selection of
    movements in connection with the environment.

6   The development of drawing skills reflects general motor devel-
    opment, the ability to perceive and abstract characteristics of

people and things, and the child's interests and creativity. Children's drawings reflect their culture, perception of reality and the particular aspects of the environment that capture their attention.

7   Motor disorders affect independent locomotion and the use of hands, as well as attachment, social participation and autonomy. While many children with severe motor impairments have other disorders, it is uncertain what is caused by neurological damage and what is due to the developmental consequences of their motor impairment.

Core Issues

• Biology and experience in motor development.
• The association between motor ability, cognition and learning disorders.

Suggestions for Further Reading

Adolph, K. E., Tamis-LeMonda, C. S., Ishak, S., Karasik, L. B., & Loboet, S. A. (2008). Locomotor experience and use of social information are posture specific. *Developmental Psychology*, *44*, 1705–1714.

Campos, J., Anderson, D. I., Barbu-Roth, M. A., Hubbard, E. M., Hertenstein, M. J., & Witherington, D. (2000). Travel broadens the mind. *Infancy*, *1*, 149–219.

Largo, R. H., Molinari, L., Weber, M., Pinto, L. C., & Duc, G. (1985). Early development of locomotion: Significance of prematurity, cerebral palsy and sex. *Developmental Medicine and Child Neurology*, *27*, 183–191.

Thelen, E. (1995). Motor development: A new synthesis. *American Psychologist*, *50*, 79–95.

von Hofsten, C. (2004). An action perspective on motor development. *Trends in Cognitive Sciences*, *8*, 266–272.

Glossary

See subject index to find the terms in the text

Accommodation Alteration or formation of a new cognitive *schema* in order to better adapt the *cognitive structure* to external conditions.

Adaptation Changes that increase the ability of a species or an individual to survive and cope with the environment.

Adolescence The period between *childhood* and adulthood, age 12–18.

Affordance According to Gibson, the relationship between the properties of the physical world and possible actions, such as perceiving an object as "graspable" or a surface as "walkable."

Associated group play Form of *group play* in which children engage in the same activities and interact to a certain degree.

Attachment A *behavioral system* that includes various forms of *attachment behavior*, the system is activated when a child finds herself at a shorter or a longer distance from the person she is attached to, and experiences emotions such as pain, fear, stress, uncertainty or anxiety; the term is also used to describe emotional attachment to a caregiver; Attachment can be secure, insecure and disorganized; see *exploration*.

Attention deficit hyperactivity disorder; ADHD Attention deficit disorder with restlessness and a high level of activity.

Atypical development Course of development that differs significantly from the development of the majority of a *population*; see *individual differences* and *typical development*.

Autism spectrum disorder Neurodevelopmental disorder that appears in the first years of life; characterized by persistent deficits in social skills, communication and language, and by repetitive behavior and restricted interests.

Automatization   Reduced conscious regulation of motor and cognitive processes as a result of repeated execution.

Autonomy   Independence, self-determination. Ability to make independent decisions related to life's everyday tasks; an important element in the formation of *identity* in *adolescence*.

Babbling   Speech-like vocalization; usually occurs at 6–7 months of age.

Babinski reflex   *Developmental reflex* elicited when a sharp object is stroked backwards along the sole of the foot, causing a child's big toe to flex upwards and the other toes to fan out; usually disappears at 8–12 months of age.

Batten disease; Juvenile neuronal ceroid lipofuscinosis (JNCL)   Genetic *autosomal* recessive disease; neurodegenerative disorder with blindness at age 5–15 and development of childhood dementia with decline in cognitive and motor functions.

Cataract   Eye disease that results in the gradual clouding of the lens.

Cerebral palsy   Impaired muscle function due to prenatal or early brain damage. Characterized by paralysis, poor motor or postural coordination, and increased or varying muscle tension.

Childhood   Age 1–12 years.

Cognition   Thinking or understanding; includes some type of perception of the world, storage in the form of mental *representation*, different ways of managing or processing new and stored experiences, and action strategies.

Cognitive structure   Complex structure of mental representations and processes that forms the basis for thoughts, actions and the perception of the outside world; evolves and changes throughout development.

Color constancy   Ability to recognize a color under different lighting conditions; see *size constancy*.

Communication   Intentional conveyance of thoughts, stories, desires, ideas, emotions, etc., to one or more persons.

Conditioning   The learning of a specific reaction in response to specific stimuli; includes classical and operant conditioning. In *classical conditioning*, a neutral stimulus is associated with an unlearned or *unconditioned stimulus* that elicits an unlearned or *unconditioned response*, eventually transforming the neutral stimulus into a conditioned stimulus that elicits a conditioned response similar to the unconditioned response. In *operant conditioning*, an action is followed by an event that increases or reduces the probability that the action will be repeated under similar circumstances*t*.

Constancy (in cognition) The ability to understand that the attributes of objects and people remain the same, even if they seem to have changed, for example due to a different viewing angle and lighting conditions; see *color constancy* and *size constancy*.

Constructive play Form of play that entails that children construct something, such as a Lego house or a clay figure; may be performed alone or together with others.

Constructivism Psychological theories based on the notion that an individual constructs his or her understanding of the outside world.

Continuity (in development) Development in which later ways of functioning build directly on previous functions and can be predicted based on them.

Core knowledge In nativist theory, the innate abilities that form the basis for further perceptual, cognitive and linguistic development.

Correspondence (cognitive) In Piaget's New Theory, the perception of structural similarity that provides a basis for comparing people, objects, events, actions, etc.

Cortex The outermost, folded layer of the brain; *phylogenetically* the most recent part of the human brain.

Culture The particular activities, tools, attitudes, beliefs, values, norms, etc., that characterize a group or a community.

Development Changes over time in the structure and functioning of human beings and animals as a result of interaction between biological and environmental factors.

Developmental disorder Disorder that is congenital or appears in *infancy* or *childhood* without the presence of external injuries or similar.

Developmental path One of several possible courses of development within the same area or domain.

Developmental reflex Early motor reflex that normally disappears within the first year of life.

Disability The difference between an individual's abilities and the demands of the environment.

Discriminate Distinguish between, react differentially.

Dishabituation Increased response to a new stimulus or aspect of a stimulus following a reduction in response intensity due to repeated presentation of a stimulus; see *habituation*.

Down syndrome; Trisomy 21 Syndrome that causes varying degrees of *intellectual disability*; caused by an error in cell division that results in a partial or complete extra copy of chromosome 21.

Dynamic system (in development) A system of nonlinear *self-organizing* and *self-regulating* processes in which qualitatively new functions occur as an *integrated* result of interaction between subsystems that may have different developmental rates.

Emotion A state caused by an event important to the person and characterized by the presence of feelings; involves physiological reactions, conscious inner experience, directed action and outward expression.

Enculturation Acquisition of a culture's practices, customs, norms, values, and the like; the first foundation in this process is children's innate social orientation.

Executive functions Cognitive functions that monitor and regulate attention and plan and supervise the execution of voluntary actions, including the inhibition to act on inappropriate impulses.

Experiment Method to test a hypothesis on specific causal relationships or connections. One or several conditions are systematically altered, and the effect is recorded. As many conditions as possible are kept constant in order not to affect the outcome, increasing the probability that the results are solely related to the conditions being studied.

Exploration According to Bowlby, a behavioral system whose function is to provide information about the environment and enable the individual to better adapt to it; activated by unfamiliar and/or complex objects; deactivated once the objects have been examined and become familiar to the individual; see *attachment* and *secure base*.

Fine motor skills Movements of the hands, fingers and toes; see *gross motor skills*.

Gender difference; Sex difference Characteristic, ability or behavior pattern that differs between the two sexes.

Gestalt principles (in perception) Principles used for perceptual organization and presumed to be innate.

Gross motor skills Movements of the body, arms and legs; see *fine motor skills*.

Habituation   Gradual reduction in the intensity of a reaction or response following repeated stimulation; allows an individual to ignore familiar objects and direct attention at new ones.

Identity   An individual's sense of who he or she is, as well as of affiliation with larger and smaller social groups and communities.

Imitation   The deliberate execution of an action to create a correspondence between what oneself does and what someone else does.

Incidence   The appearance of new occurrences of a trait, disease or similar in a particular *population* during a particular time span, often expressed as the number of incidences per 1,000 individuals per year; see *prevalence*.

Individual differences   Variation in skills and characteristics between the individuals in a *population*; see *atypical development* and *typical development*.

Infancy   The first year of life.

Integration (in development)   Coordination; progress toward greater organization and a more complex structure.

Intellectual disability; Learning disability; Mental retardation   Significant problems learning and adjusting that affect most areas of functioning; graded mild (IQ 70–50), moderate (IQ 49–35), severe (IQ 34–20) and profound (IQ below 20); in clinical contexts, a significant reduction in social adjustment is an additional criterion.

Intermodal perception   Perception of a person, an event or an object whereby information from two or more senses is combined, for example seeing and hearing a cat meow.

Intonation   The melody or pattern of changes in the pitch of the speaking voice.

Joint attention   Two or more individuals share a common focus of attention, while at the same time being aware that the same focus of attention is shared by the other person(s).

Language functioning   The purpose of speech; the objective one wants to achieve by conveying something to another person using language.

Learned helplessness   The experience of lacking self-determination and the ability to affect one's environment as a result of having experienced situations in which one felt little control.

Learning   Relatively permanent change in understanding and behavior as the result of experience; see *development* and *maturation*.

Learning disorder   Significant problems developing skills in a specific area of knowledge, such as language impairment, reading/writing disorders (*dyslexia*) and difficulties with math (dyscalculia); often referred to as specific learning disorder as opposed to general learning disability; see *intellectual disability*.

Maturation   Developmental change caused by genetically determined regulating mechanisms that are relatively independent of the individual's specific experiences; see *development* and *learning*.

Mental disorder   Behavioral or psychological pattern that occurs in an individual and leads to clinically significant distress or impairment in one or more important areas of functioning.

Mind understanding   Understanding that other people have internal states, such as knowledge, feelings and plans, that may be different from one's own and may affect their actions; see *theory of mind*.

Module (in cognition)   Isolated brain system that deals with a particular type of stimulation and knowledge.

Moro reflex   *Developmental reflex* elicited when an infant extends her arms and the head suddenly loses support, causing the infant's arms to move toward the body's midline; usually disappears at 5–6 months of age.

Neuronal group selection, theory of   Theory of motor development based on the assumption that evolution has resulted in a structure of primary neuronal groups (nerve cell connections) that control motor functions and changes with experience, i.e. that information from the muscles affects the development of the brain.

Norm (in a test)   A standard or normative score for a certain age level, based on the results from a large number of individuals.

Object (in psychodynamic theory)   Mental representation of a person or an object that is the goal of a drive, or through which a drive can achieve its goal.

Observational learning   Learning by observing the behavior of others and the consequences of their behavior.

Palmar grasp reflex   *Developmental reflex* causing the fingers to flex inward when the infant's palm is gently touched; usually disappears at 2–4 months of age.

Perception   Knowledge gained through the senses; discernment, selection and processing of sensory input.

Personality   An individual's characteristic tendency to feel, think and act in specific ways.

Pincer grip   Grip of the thumb and index finger.

Plantar reflex   *Developmental reflex* that causes the toes to flex inward when the ball of the foot is stimulated; usually disappears at 9–10 months of age.

Population (in statistics)   The sum total of individuals, objects, events and the like included in a study. Also used to describe a group of individuals with a common measurable attribute, such as children in a certain school grade or young people in cities.

Preference for novelty   Tendency to be more attentive to new rather than familiar stimulation; appears in infants after the age of 3 months.

Preschool age   Age 3–6 years.

Prevalence   Relative presence of for example traits, diseases and syndromes in a particular population at a certain time; see *incidence*.

Recognition   The process of experiencing something in the moment that has been experienced before, such as when children consciously or nonconsciously show that they have seen a particular image before.

Reflective abstraction   According to Piaget, knowledge acquired by thinking about one's own thoughts and forming abstractions based on these personal reflections; see *cognitive structure*.

Reflex   Unlearned and involuntary response to an external stimulus.

Rooting reflex   *Developmental reflex* elicited when an infant is lightly touched on the cheek and turns the head toward the side being stimulated; usually disappears at 3 months of age.

School age   Age 6–12.

Self-evaluation; Self-esteem   The assessment of one's own characteristics in relation to an inner standard that includes how and who one wishes to be; can also refer to questionnaires, surveys and the like about a person's characteristics.

Self-image   Positive or negative perception of oneself and one's own characteristics.

Self-organizing   The emergence or establishment of new structures not driven by external factors.

Self-regulation   The ability to monitor and adapt one's own thoughts, feelings, reactions and actions in order to cope with the requirements, challenges and opportunities of the environment and be able to achieve one's goals; also referred to as self-control.

Sensory modality   One of several specific senses, such as vision or hearing.

Sign language Visual-manual language, primarily using movements of the arms, hands and fingers, supported by body movements, mouth movements and facial gestures.

Size constancy Ability to perceive the size of an object as constant despite changes in the size of the image projected on the retina; see *color constancy* and *constancy*.

Social referencing Using other people's emotional reactions to evaluate uncertain situations.

Stage (in development) Delimited period of time in which thoughts, feelings and behavior are organized in a way that is qualitatively different from the preceding or following periods.

Stereoscopic vision Ability to perceive space as three-dimensional due to a small difference between the images that are projected on the retina when the eyes are directed at the same point (parallax).

Syndrome Set of attributes and behavioral characteristics that regularly occur together.

Test Measurement instrument; a collection of questions or tasks that provide a basis for assessing an individual's performance relative to peers or a specific set of criteria.

Theory of mind The understanding that human beings are thinking and sentient beings who act according to how they perceive a given situation; see *mind understanding*.

Typical development Course of development that characterizes the majority of a *population*; see *atypical development* and *individual differences*.

Visual perspective Ability to understand what others are able or unable to see.

Bibliography

Adolph, K. E., & Robinson, S. R. (2015). Motor development. In R. M. Lerner, L. Liben & U. Muller (Eds), *Handbook of child psychology and developmental science, Seventh edition, Volume 2: Cognitive processes* (pp. 114–157). New York, NY: Wiley.

Adolph, K. E., & Tamis-LeMonda, C. S. (2014). The costs and benefits of development: The transition from crawling to walking. *Child Development Perspectives, 8*, 187–192.

Andersen, G. L., Irgens, L. M., Haagaas, I., Skranes, J. S., Meberg, A. E., & Vik, T. (2008). Cerebral palsy in Norway: Prevalence, subtypes and severity. *European Journal of Paediatric Neurology, 12*, 4–13.

Anderson, D. I., Campos, J. J., Rivera, M., Dahl, A., Uchiyama, I., & Barbu-Roth, M. (2014). The consequences of independent locomotion for brain and psychological development. In R. B. Shepherd (Ed.), *Cerebral palsy in infancy* (pp. 199–223). Edinburgh, UK: Elsevier.

Arnheim, R. (1974). *Art and visual perception: A psychology of the creative eye.* Berkeley, CA: University of California Press.

Aronsson, K. (1997). *Barns världar–barns bilder.* Stockholm, Sweden: Natur och Kultur.

Bahrick, L. E. (2004). The development of perception in a multimodal environment. In G. Bremner & A. Slater (Eds), *Theories of infant development* (pp. 90–120). Malden, MA: Blackwell.

Bahrick, L. E., & Lickliter, R. (2000). Intersensory redundancy guides attentional selectivity and perceptual learning in infancy. *Developmental Psychology, 36*, 190–201.

Bahrick, L. E., & Lickliter, R. (2014). Learning to attend selectively: The dual role of intersensory redundancy. *Current Directions in Psychological Science, 23*, 414–420.

Bahrick, L. E., Walker, A. S., & Neisser, U. (1981). Selective looking by infants. *Cognitive Psychology, 13*, 377–390.

Balogh, R. D., & Porter, R. H. (1986). Olfactory preferences resulting from mere exposure in human neonates. *Infant Behavior and Development, 9*, 395–401.

Banihani, R., Smile, S., Yoon, G., Dupuis, A., Mosleh, M., Snider, A., & McAdam, L. (2015). Cognitive and neuro-behavioral profile in boys with Duchenne muscular dystrophy. *Journal of Child Neurology, 30,* 1472–1482.

Bar-Haim, Y., Ziv, T., Lamy, D., & Hodes, R. (2006). Nature and nurture in own-race face processing. *Psychological Science, 17,* 159–163.

Becker, F., & Erlenkamp, S. (2007). Et språkløst liv med cochleaimplantat? *Tidsskrift for Norsk Lægeforening, 127,* 2836–2838.

Bertenthal, B. I., & Clifton, R. K. (1998). Perception and action. In W. Damon, D. Kuhn & R. S. Siegler (Eds), *Handbook of child psychology, Fifth edition, Volume 2: Cognition, perception, and language* (pp. 51–102). New York, NY: Wiley.

Biringen, Z., Emde, R. N., Campos, J. J., & Appelbaum, A. (2008). Development of autonomy: Role of walking onset and its timing. *Perceptual and Motor Skills, 106,* 395–414.

Bjørgaas, H. M., Hysing, M., & Elgen, I. (2012). Psychiatric disorders among children with cerebral palsy at school starting age. *Research in Developmental Disabilities, 33,* 1287–1293.

Blair, E. (2010). Epidemiology of the cerebral palsies. *Orthopedic Clinics of North America, 41,* 441–455.

Blakemore, C., & Cooper, G. F. (1970). Development of the brain depends on the visual environment. *Nature, 228,* 477–478.

Bornstein, M. H. (1992). Perception across the life span. In M. H. Bornstein & M. E. Lamb (Eds), *Developmental psychology: An advanced textbook, Third edition* (pp. 155–209). Hillsdale, NJ: Lawrence Erlbaum.

Brambring, M. (2007). Divergent development of manual skills in children who are blind or sighted. *Journal of Visual Impairment & Blindness, 101* (4), 212–225.

Bremner, G. (1997). From perception to cognition. In G. Bremner, A. Slater & G. Butterworth (Eds). *Infant development: Recent advances* (pp. 55–74). Hove, UK: Lawrence Erlbaum.

Britten, K. H. (2008). Mechanisms of self-motion perception. *Annual Review of Neuroscience, 31,* 389–410.

Brossard-Racine, M., Hall, N., Majnemer, A., Shevell, M. I., Law, M., Poulin, C., & Rosenbaum, P. (2012). Behavioural problems in school age children with cerebral palsy. *European Journal of Paediatric Neurology, 16,* 35–41.

Bushnell, I. W., Sai, F., & Mullin, J. T. (1989). Neonatal recognition of the mother's face. *British Journal of Developmental Psychology, 7,* 3–15.

Campos, J. J., Anderson, D. I., Barbu-Roth, M. A., Hubbard, E. M., Hertenstein, M. J., & Witherington, D. (2000). Travel broadens the mind. *Infancy, 1,* 149–219.

Carbon, C. C. (2014). Understanding human perception by human-made illusions. *Frontiers in Human Neuroscience, 8,* 566.

Carey, S. (1996). Perceptual classification and expertise. In R. Gelman & T.K.-F. Au (Eds), *Perceptual and cognitive development* (pp. 49–69). London: Academic Press.

Carney, R. N., & Levin, J. R. (2002). Pictorial illustrations still improve students' learning from text. *Educational Psychology Review, 14,* 5–26.

Carruth, B. R., Ziegler, P. J., Gordon, A., & Barr, S.I. (2004). Prevalence of picky eaters among infants and toddlers and their caregivers' decisions about offering a new food. *Journal of the American Dietetic Association, 104* (Supplement 1), S57–S64.

Cernoch, J. M., & Porter, R. H. (1985). Recognition of maternal axillary odors by infants. *Child Development, 56,* 1593–1598.

Chang, H.-W., & Trehub, S. E. (1977). Auditory processing of relational information by young infants. *Journal of Experimental Child Psychology, 24,* 324–331.

Chatterjee, M., Zion, D. J., Deroche, M. L., Burianek, B. A., Limb, C. J., Goren, A. P., Kulkarni, A. M., & Christensen, J. A. (2015). Voice emotion recognition by cochlear-implanted children and their normally-hearing peers. *Hearing Research, 322,* 151–162.

Condry, K. F., Smith, W. C., & Spelke, E. S. (2001). Development of perceptual organization. In F. Lacerda, C. von Hofsten & M. Heimann (Eds), *Emerging cognitive abilities in early infancy* (pp. 1–28). Mahwah, NJ: Erlbaum.

Connolly, K. J., & Dalgleish, M. (1993). Individual patterns of tool use by infants. In A. F. Kalverboer, B. Hopkins & R. Geuze (Eds), *Motor development in early and later childhood: Longitudinal approaches* (pp. 174–204). Cambridge: Cambridge University Press.

Constable, H., Campbell, B., & Brown, R. (1988). Sectional drawings from science textbooks: An experimental investigation into pupil's understanding. *British Journal of Educational Psychology, 58,* 89–102.

Cook, M. (2008). Students' comprehension of science concepts depicted in textbook illustrations. *Electronic Journal of Science Education, 12,* 1–14.

Cox, D. R., Skinner, J. D., Carruth, B. R., Moran, J., & Houck, K. S. (1997). A food variety index for toddlers (VIT): Development and application. *Journal of the American Dietetic Association, 97,* 1382–1386.

Dahlgren Sandberg, A. (2006). Reading and spelling abilities in children with severe speech impairments and cerebral palsy at 6, 9, and 12 years of age in relation to cognitive development: A longitudinal study. *Developmental Medicine and Child Neurology, 48,* 629–634.

Dakin, S., & Frith, U. (2005). Vagaries of visual perception in autism. *Neuron, 48,* 497–507.

DeLoache, J. S. (1987). Rapid change in the symbolic functioning of very young children. *Science, 238,* 1556–1557.

DeLoache, J. S., & Burns, N. M. (1994). Early understanding of the representational function of pictures. *Cognition, 52,* 83–110.

DeLoache, J. S., Strauss, M., & Maynard. J. (1979). Picture perception in infancy. *Infant Behavior and Development, 2,* 77–89.

Deocampo, J. A., & Hudson, J. A. (2005). When seeing is not believing: Two-year-olds' use of video representations to find a hidden toy. *Journal of Cognition and Development, 6,* 229–260.

Dilks, D. D., Hoffman, J. E., & Landau, B. (2008). Vision for perception and vision for action: Normal and unusual development. *Developmental Science, 11,* 474–486.

Doherty, M. J., Anderson, J. R., & Howieson, L. (2009). The rapid development of explicit gaze judgment ability at 3 years. *Journal of Experimental Child Psychology, 104,* 296–312.

Doherty, M. J., Tsuji, H., & Phillips, W. A. (2008). The context-sensitivity of visual size perception varies across cultures. *Perception, 37,* 1426–1433.

Durand, K., Baudon, G., Freydefont, L., & Schaal, B. (2008). Odorization of a novel object can influence infant's exploratory behavior in unexpected ways. *Infant Behavior and Development, 31,* 629–636.

Edelman, G. M. (1989). *Neural Darwinism. The theory of neuronal group selection.* Oxford: Oxford University Press.

Elkind, D., Koegler, R. R., & Go, E. (1964). Studies in perceptual development: II Part-whole perception. *Child Development, 35,* 81–90.

Fagan, J. F. (1979). The origin of facial pattern perception. In M. H. Bornstein & W. Kessen (Eds), *Psychological development from infancy: Image to intention* (pp. 83–113). Hillsdale, NJ: Lawrence Erlbaum.

Fantz, R. L. (1958). Pattern vision in young infants. *Psychological Record, 8,* 43–47.

Fantz, R. L. (1961). The origin of form perception. *Scientific American, 204,* 66–72.

Fantz, R. L., & Fagan, J. F. (1975). Visual attention to size and number of pattern details by term and preterm infants during the first six months. *Child Development, 46,* 3–18.

Fantz, R. L., & Miranda, S. B. (1975). Newborn infant attention to form of contour. *Child Development, 46,* 224–228.

Fazzi, E., Lanners, J., Ferrari-Ginevra, O., Achille, C., Luparia, A., Signorini, S., & Lanzi, G. (2002). Gross motor development and reach on sound as critical tools for the development of the blind child. *Brain Development, 24,* 269–275.

Fazzi, E., Signorini, S. G., Bomba, M., Luparia, A., Lanners, J., & Balottin, U. (2011). Reach on sound: A key to object permanence in visually impaired children. *Early Human Development, 87,* 289–296.

Ferdenzi, C., Coureaud, G., Camos, V., & Schaal, B. (2008). Human awareness and uses of odor cues in everyday life: Results from a questionnaire study in children. *International Journal of Behavioral Development, 32,* 417–426.

Ferguson, K. T., Kulkofsky, S., Cashon, C. H., & Casasola, M. (2009). The development of specialized processing of own-race faces in infancy. *Infancy*, *14*, 263–284.

Fifer, W. P., & Moon, C. M. (1995). The effects of experience with fetal sound. In J.-P. Lecanuet, W. P. Fifer, N. A. Krasnegor & W. P. Smotherman (Eds), *Fetal development* (pp. 351–366). Hove, UK: Lawrence Erlbaum.

Fraiberg, S. (1977). *Insights from the blind*. New York, NY: Basic Books.

Freedman, D. A., & Cannady, C. (1971). Delayed emergence of prone locomotion. *Journal of Nervous and Mental Disease*, *153*, 108–117.

Fukushima, S. (2011). The deafblind and disability studies. In A. Matsui, O. Nagase, A. Sheldon, D. Goodley & Y. Sawada (Eds), *Creating a society for all: Disability and economy* (pp. 50–58). Leeds, UK: The Disability Press.

Gallahue, D. L., & Ozmun, J. C. (1997). *Understanding motor development: Infants, children, adolescents and adults, Fourth edition*. Boston, MA: McGraw-Hill.

Gallahue, D. L., & Ozmun, J. C. (2006). *Understanding motor development: Infants, children, adolescents, adults, Sixth edition*. Boston, MA: McGraw-Hill.

Gardner, H. (1993). *Multiple intelligences: The theory in practice*. New York, NY: Basic Books.

Geddie, B. E., Bina, M. J., Miller, M. M., Bathshaw, M. L., Roizen, N. J., & Lotrecchiano, G. R. (2013). Vision and visual impairment. In G. Lotrecchiano, N. Roizen & M. Batshaw (Eds), *Children with disabilities, Seventh edition* (pp. 169–188). Baltimore, MD: Brookes.

Geers, A. E., Moog, J. S., Biedenstein, J., Brenner, C., & Hayes, H. (2009). Spoken language scores of children using cochlear implants compared to hearing age-mates at school entry. *The Journal of Deaf Studies and Deaf Education*, *14*, 371–385.

Gesell, A., & Thompson, H. (1929). Learning and growth in identical infant twins. *Genetic Psychology Monographs*, *6*, 1–124.

Gibson, E. J. (1982). The concept of affordances in development: The renaissance of functionalism. In W. A. Collins, *Minnesota symposia on child psychology, Volume 15* (pp. 55–81). Hillsdale, NJ: Erlbaum.

Gibson, E. J., Riccio, G., Schmuckler, M. A., Stoffregen, T. A., Rosenberg, D., & Taormina, J. (1987). Detection of the traversability of surfaces by crawling and walking infants. *Journal of Experimental Psychology: Human Perception and Performance*, *13*, 533–544.

Gibson, E. J., & Walk, R. D. (1960). The "visual cliff". *Scientific American, 202*, 64–71.

Gibson, J. J. (1979). *The ecological approach to visual perception*. Boston: Houghton Mifflin.

Goldfield, E. C., & Wolff, P. H. (2004). A dynamical systems perspective on infant action and its development. In G. Bremner & A. Slater (Eds), *Theories of infant development* (pp. 3–29). Oxford: Blackwell.

Goren, C. C., Sarty, M., & Wu, P. (1975). Visual following and pattern discrimination of face-like stimuli by newborn infants. *Pediatrics, 56,* 544–545.

Gottlieb, G., Wahlsten, D., & Lickliter, R. (2006). The significance of biology for human development: A developmental psychobiological systems view. In R. W. Damon & R. M. Lerner (Eds), *Handbook of child development, Sixth edition, Volume 1: Theoretical models of human development* (pp. 210–257). New York, NY: Wiley.

Granrud, C. E., & Schmechel, T. T. N. (2006). Development of size constancy in children: A test of the proximal mode sensitivity hypothesis. *Perception and Psychophysics, 68,* 1372–1381.

Gudgeon, S., & Kirk, S. (2015). Living with a powered wheelchair: Exploring children's and young people's experiences, *Disability and Rehabilitation: Assistive Technology, 10,* 118–125.

Hadders-Algra, M. (2002). Variability in infant motor behavior: A hallmark of the healthy nervous system. *Infant Behavior and Development, 25,* 433–451.

Hannon, E. E., & Johnson, S. P. (2005). Infants use meter to categorize rhythms and melodies: Implications for musical structure learning. *Cognitive Psychology, 50,* 354–377.

Happé, F. G. E. (1996). Studying weak central coherence at low levels: Children with autism do not succumb to visual illusions. A research note. *Journal of Child Psychology and Psychiatry, 37,* 873–877.

Hargreaves, D. J. (1986). *The developmental psychology of music.* Cambridge: Cambridge University Press.

Harris, G. (1997). Development of taste perception and appetite regulation. In G. Bremner, A. Slater & G. Butterworth (Eds), *Infant development: Recent advances* (pp. 9–30). Hove, UK: Erlbaum.

Harris, P. L., Kavanaugh, R. D., & Dowson, L. (1997). The depiction of imaginary transformations: Early comprehension of a symbolic function. *Cognitive Development, 12,* 1–19.

Held, R., & Hein, A. (1963). Movement produced stimulation in the development of visually guided behavior. *Journal of Comparative and Physiological Psychology, 56,* 872–876.

Hetland, L. (2000). Listening to music enhances spatial–temporal reasoning: Evidence for the 'Mozart Effect'. *Journal of Aesthetic Education, 34,* 105–148.

Hobson, P. R., & Bishop, M. (2003). The pathogenesis of autism: Insights from congenital blindness. *Philosophical Transactions of the Royal Society B: Biological Sciences, 358 (1430),* 335–344.

Hochberg, J., & Brooks, V. (1962). Pictorial recogniton as an unlearned ability: A study of one child's performance. *American Journal of Psychology, 75,* 624–628.

Hodge, S., & Eccles, F. (2013). *Loneliness, social isolation and sight loss.* London: Thomas Pocklington Trust.

Holle, B. (1981). *Læse/skrive parat?* Copenhagen, DK: Munksgaard.

Holm, A. M., & Thau, L. (1984). *Børns billedverden.* Copenhagen, DK: Børn & Unge.

Hopkins, B., Beek, P. J., & Kalverboer, A. F. (1993). Theoretical issues in the longitudinal study of motor development. In A. F. Kalverboer, B. Hopkins & R. Geuze (Eds), *Motor development in early and later childhood: Longitudinal approaches* (pp. 343–371). Cambridge: Cambridge University Press.

Hopkins, B., & Butterworth, G. (1997). Dynamical systems approaches to development of action. In G. Bremner, A. Slater & G. Butterworth (Eds), *Infant development: Recent advances* (pp. 75–100). Hove, UK: Lawrence Erlbaum.

Howe, M. J. A., Davidson, J. W., & Sloboda, J. A. (1998). Innate talents: Reality or myth? *Behavioral and Brain Sciences, 21,* 399–407.

Hutt, S. J., Hutt, C., Lenard, H. G., von Bernuth, H., & Muntjewerff, W. J. (1968). Auditory responsivity in the human neonate. *Nature, 218,* 888–890.

Iverson, J. M. (2010). Developing language in a developing body: The relationship between motor development and language development. *Journal of Child Language, 37,* 229–261.

James, W. (1890). *The principles of psychology.* New York, NY: Holt.

Jersild, A. T., & Bienstock, S. F. (1935). *Development of rhythm in young children. Child Development Monographs, number 22.* New York, NY: Teachers College, Columbia University.

Johnson, M. H., Dziurawiec, S., Ellis, H. D., & Morton, J. (1991). Newborns' preferential tracking of face-like stimuli and its subsequent decline. *Cognition, 40,* 1–19.

Johnson, S. P. (2004). Development of perceptual completion in infancy. *Psychological Science, 15,* 769–775.

Johnson, S. P. (2005). Building knowledge from perception in infancy. In L. Gershkoff-Stowe & D. Rakison (Eds), *Building object categories in developmental time* (pp. 33–62). Mahwah, NJ: Erlbaum.

Johnson, S. P., & Hannon, E. E. (2015). Perceptual development. In L. S. Liben, U. Müller & R. M. Lerner (Eds), *Handbook of child psychology and developmental science, Seventh edition, Volume 2: Cognitive processes* (pp. 63–112). Hoboken, NJ: Wiley.

Kagan, J. (2008). In defense of qualitative changes in development. *Child Development, 79,* 1606–1624.

Káldy, Z., & Kovács, I. (2003). Visual context integration is not fully developed in 4-year-old children. *Perception, 32,* 657–666.

Karayanidis, F., Kelly, M., Chapman, P., Mayes, A., & Johnston, P. (2009). Facial identity and facial expression matching in 5–12-year-old children and adults. *Infant and Child Development, 18,* 404–421.

Kavšek, M., Granrud, C. E., & Yonas, A. (2009). Infants' responsiveness to pictorial depth cues in preferential-reaching studies: A meta-analysis. *Infant Behavior and Development, 32,* 245–253.

Kellman, P. J. (1996). The origins of object perception. In R. Gelman & T. K. F. Au (Eds), *Perceptual and cognitive development* (pp. 3–48). London: Academic Press.

Kellman, P. J., & Spelke, E. S. (1983). Perception of partly occluded objects in infancy. *Cognitive Psychology, 15,* 483–524.

Kelly, D. J., Liu, S., Lee, K., Quinn, P. C., Pascalis, O., Slater, A. M., & Ge, L. (2009). Development of the other-race effect in infancy: Evidence towards universality? *Journal of Experimental Child Psychology, 104,* 105–114.

Kesiktas, A. D. (2009). Early childhood special education for children with visual impairments: Problems and solutions. *Educational Sciences: Theory and Practice, 9,* 823–832.

Kestenbaum, R., Termine, N., & Spelke, E. S. (1987). Perception of objects and object boundaries by three-month-old infants. *British Journal of Developmental Psychology, 5,* 361–383.

Kinzler, K. D., & Spelke, E. S. (2007). Core systems in human cognition. *Progress in Brain Research, 164,* 257–264.

Konner, M. J. (1976). Maternal care, infant behavior and development among the !Kung. In R. B. Lee & I. DeVore (Eds), *Kalahari hunter-gatherers: Studies of the !Kung San and their neighbors* (pp. 218–245). Cambridge, MA: Harvard University Press.

Kovács, I. (2000). Human development of perceptual organization. *Vision Research, 40,* 1301–1310.

Kretch, K. S., Franchak, J. M., & Adolph, K. E. (2014). Crawling and walking infants see the world differently. *Child Development, 85,* 1503–1518.

Kuppler, K., Lewis, M., & Evans, A. K. (2013). A review of unilateral hearing loss and academic performance: Is it time to reassess traditional dogmata? *International Journal of Pediatric Otorhinolaryngology, 77,* 617–622.

Landau, B., & Gleitman, L. R. (1985). *Language and experience: Evidence from the blind child.* Cambridge, MA: Harvard University Press.

Lang-Roth, R. (2014). Hearing impairment and language delay in infants: Diagnostics and genetics. *GMS Current Topics in Otorhinolaryngology, Head and Neck Surgery, 13,* 05.

Largo, R. H., Molinari, L., Weber, M., Pinto, L. C., & Duc, G. (1985). Early development of locomotion: Significance of prematurity, cerebral palsy and sex. *Developmental Medicine and Child Neurology, 27,* 183–191.

Largo, R. H., Caflisch, J. A., Hug, F., Muggli, K., Molnar, A. A., & Molinari, L. (2001b). Neuromotor development from 5 to 18 years. Part 2: Associated movements. *Developmental Medicine and Child Neurology, 43,* 444–453.

Largo, R. H., Caflisch, J. A., Hug, F., Muggli, K., Molnar, A. A., Molinari, L., Sheehy, A., Gasser, T. (2001a). Neuromotor development from 5 to 18 years.

Part 1: Timed performance. *Developmental Medicine and Child Neurology*, *43*, 436–443.

Lederberg, A. R., Schick, B., & Spencer, P. E. (2013). Language and literacy development of deaf and hard-of-hearing children: Successes and challenges. *Developmental Psychology*, *49*, 15–30.

Leibold, L. J. (2012). Development of auditory scene analysis and auditory attention. In L. A. Werner, A. N. Popper & R. R. Fay (Eds), *Human auditory development* (pp. 137–161). New York, NY: Springer.

Lewis, T. L., & Maurer, D. (2005). Multiple sensitive periods in human visual development: Evidence from visually deprived children. *Developmental Psychobiology*, *46*, 163–183.

Lewis, T. L., & Maurer, D. (2009). Effects of early pattern deprivation on visual development. *Optometry and Vision Science*, *86*, 640–646.

Lewkowicz, D. J. (1994). Development of intersensory perception in human infants. In D. J. Lewkowicz & R. Lickliter (Eds), *The development of intersensory perception: Comparative perspectives* (pp. 165–203). Hillsdale, NJ: Erlbaum.

Lieu, J. E., Tye-Murray, N., & Fu, Q. (2012). Longitudinal study of children with unilateral hearing loss. *The Laryngoscope*, *122*, 2088–2095.

Luquet, G. H. (1927). *Le dessin enfantin*. Paris: Alcan.

Lynch, M. P., & Eilers, R. E. (1992). A study of perceptual development for musical tuning. *Perception and Psychophysics*, *52*, 599–608.

Madge, N., & Fassam, M. (1982). *Ask the children. Experiences of physical disability in the school years*. London: Batsford.

Martlew, M., & Connolly, K. J. (1996). Human figure drawings by schooled and unschooled children in Papua New Guinea. *Child Development*, *67*, 2743–2762.

Masataka, N. (2006). Preference for consonance over dissonance by hearing newborns of deaf parents and of hearing parents. *Developmental Science*, *9*, 46–50.

McGraw, M. B. (1943). *The neuromuscular maturation of the human infant*. New York, NY: Columbia University Press.

McKelvie, P., & Low, J. (2002). Listening to Mozart does not improve children's spatial ability: Final curtains for the Mozart Effect. *British Journal of Developmental Psychology*, *20*, 241–258.

Mehler, J., Bertoncini, J., Barriere, M., & Jassik-Gerschenfeld, D. (1978). Infant recognition of mother's voice. *Perception*, *7*, 491–497.

Miller, L. K. (1989). *Musical savants: Exceptional skills in the mentally retarded*. Hillsdale, NJ: Erlbaum.

Mitchell, R. E., & Karchmer, M. A. (2004). Chasing the mythical ten percent: Parental hearing status of deaf and hard of hearing students in the United States. *Sign Language Studies*, *4*, 138–163.

Moog, H. (1963). *Beginn und erste Entwicklung des Musikerlebens im Kindesalter: Eine empirisch-psychologishe Untersuchung*. Dissertation, University of Cologne.

Morrongiello, B. A. (1990). The study of individual differences in infants: Auditory processing measures. In J. Colombo & J. W. Fagen (Eds), *Individual differences in infancy: Reliability, stability, prediction* (pp. 271–320). Hillsdale, NJ: Erlbaum.

Mullin, J. (2014). *Drawing autism.* New York, NY: Akashic Books.

Nafstad, A., & Rødbroe, I. (2016). *Communicative relations.* Aalborg, Denmark: Materialecentret.

Nanez, J. E. (1988). Perception of impending collision in 3- to 6-week-old human infants. *Infant Behavior and Development, 11,* 447–463.

Neil, P. A., Chee-Ruiter, C., Scheier, C., Lewkowicz, D. J., & Shimojo, S. (2006). Development of multisensory spatial integration and perception in humans. *Developmental Science, 9,* 454–464.

Nelson, D. K., O'Neill, K., & Asher, Y. M. (2008). A mutually facilitative relationship between learning names and learning concepts in preschool children: The case of artifacts. *The Journal of Cognition and Development, 9,* 171–193.

Nicklaus, S. (2009). Development of food variety in children. *Appetite, 52,* 53–55.

Nicklaus, S., Boggio, V., Chabanet, C., & Issanchou, S. (2005). A prospective study of food variety seeking in childhood, adolescence and early adult life. *Appetite, 44,* 289–297.

Odding, E., Roebroeck, M. E., & Stam, H. J. (2006). The epidemiology of cerebral palsy: Incidence, impairments and risk factors. *Disability and Rehabilitation, 28,* 183–191.

Olsho, L. W., Koch, E. G., & Halpin, C. F. (1987). Level and age effects in infant frequency discrimination. *The Journal of the Acoustical Society of America, 82,* 454–464.

Peretz, I., & Hyde, K. L. (2003). What is specific to music processing? Insights from congenital amusia. *Trends in Cognitive Sciences, 7,* 362–367.

Pérez-Pereira, M. (2014). Contrasting views on the pragmatic abilities of blind children. *Enfance, 2014,* 73–88.

Pérez-Pereira, M., & Conti-Ramsden, G. (1999). *Language development and social interaction in blind children.* Hove, UK: Psychology Press.

Piaget, J. (1952). *The origin of intelligence in the child.* London: Routledge and Kegan Paul.

Picci, G., & Scherf, K. S. (2016). From caregivers to peers: Puberty shapes human face perception. *Psychological Science, 27,* 1461–1473.

Piek, J. P. (2002). The role of variability in early motor development. *Infant Behavior and Development, 25,* 452–465.

Piper, M. C., & Darrah, J. (1994). *Motor assessment of the developing infant.* Philadelphia, PA: W. B. Saunders.

Plantinga, J., & Trehub, S. E. (2014). Revisiting the innate preference for consonance. *Journal of Experimental Psychology: Human Perception and Performance, 40,* 40–49.

Povinelli, D. J., Landry, A. M., Theall, L. A., Clark, B. R., & Castille, C. M. (1999). Development of young children's understanding that the recent past is causally bound to the present. *Developmental Psychology, 35,* 1426–1439.

Prechtl, H. F. R. (1993). Principles of early motor development in the human. In A. F. Kalverboer, B. Hopkins & R. Geuze (Eds), *Motor development in early and later childhood: Longitudinal approaches* (pp. 35–50). Cambridge: Cambridge University Press.

Quinn, P. C. (2006). On the emergence of perceptual organization and categorization in young infants: Roles for perceptual process and knowledge access. In L. Balter & C. Tamis-Le Monda (Eds), *Child psychology: A handbook of contemporary issues, Second edition* (pp. 109–131). Philadelphia, PA: Psychology Press.

Quinn, P. C., Bhatt, R. S., Brush, D., Grimes, A., & Sharpnack, H. (2002). Development of form similarity as a Gestalt grouping principle in infancy. *Psychological Science, 13,* 320–328.

Quinn, P. C., Lee, K., Pascalis, O., & Tanaka, J. W. (2016). Narrowing in categorical responding to other-race face classes by infants. *Developmental Science, 19,* 362–371.

Raskin, L. A., Maital, S., & Bornstein, M. H. (1983). Perceptual categorization of color: A life span study. *Psychological Research, 45,* 135–145.

Rauscher, F. H., & Hinton, S. C. (2006). The Mozart effect: Music listening is not music instruction. *Educational Psychologist, 41,* 233–238.

Rauscher, F. H., Shaw, G. L., & Ky, K. N. (1993). Music and spatial task performance. *Nature, 365,* 611.

Riesen, A. H. (1947). The development of visual perception in man and chimpanzee. *Science, 106,* 107–108.

Robinson, C. W., & Sloutsky, V. M. (2004). Auditory dominance and its change in the course of development. *Child Development, 75,* 1387–1401.

Rochat, P. (1993). Hand mouth coordination in the newborn: Morphology, determinants, and early development of a basic act. In G. J. P. Savelsbergh (Ed.), *The development of coordination in infancy* (pp. 265–288). Amsterdam, NL: North Holland/Elsevier.

Roe, J. (2008). Social inclusion: Meeting the socio-emotional needs of children with vision needs. *British Journal of Visual Impairment, 26,* 147–158.

Ropar, D., & Mitchell, P. (2001). Susceptibility to illusions and performance on visuospatial tasks in individuals with autism. *Journal of Child Psychology and Psychiatry, 42,* 539–549.

Rosander, K., & von Hofsten, C. (2004). Infants' emerging ability to represent occluded object motion. *Cognition, 91,* 1–22.

Rose, S. A., & Ruff, H. A. (1987). Cross modal abilities in human infants. In J. D. Osofsky (Ed.), *Handbook of infant development, Second edition* (pp. 318–362). New York, NY: John Wiley.

Rosenstein, D., & Oster, H. (1988). Differential facial responses to four basic tastes in newborns. *Child Development, 59*, 1555–1568.

Rozin, P. (1989). Disorders of food selection: The compromise of pleasure. In L. H. Schneider, S. J. Cooper & K. A. Halmi (Eds), *The psychobiology of human eating disorders: Preclinical and clinical perspectives* (pp. 376–386). New York, NY: New York Academy of Sciences.

Ruff, H. A. (1984). Infants' manipulative exploration of objects: Effects of age and object characteristics. *Developmental Psychology, 20*, 9–20.

Sai, F. Z. (2005). The role of the mother's voice in developing mother's face preference: Evidence for intermodal perception at birth. *Infant and Child Development, 14*, 29–50.

Salminen, A. L., & Karhula, M. E. (2014). Young persons with visual impairment: Challenges of participation. *Scandinavian Journal of Occupational Therapy, 21*, 267–276.

Sameroff, A. J. (Ed.) (2009). *The transactional model of development: How children and contexts shape each other.* Washington, DC: American Psychological Association.

Schmuckler, M. A. (2013). Perceptual-motor relations in obvious and non-obvious domains: A history and review. In P. D. Zelazo (Ed.), *Oxford handbook of developmental psychology* (pp. 237–270). Oxford: Oxford University Press.

Scott, L. S., Pascalis, O., & Nelson, C. A. (2007). A domaingeneral theory of the development of perceptual discrimination. *Current Directions in Psychological Science, 16*, 197–201.

Shuter-Dyson, R., & Gabriel, C. (1981). *The psychology of musical ability.* London: Methuen.

Sigurdardottir, S., Eiriksdottir, A., Gunnarsdottir, E., Meintema, M., Arnadottir, U., & Vik, T. (2008). Cognitive profile in young Icelandic children with cerebral palsy. *Developmental Medicine and Child Neurology, 50*, 357–362.

Simcock, G., & DeLoache, J. S. (2006). Get the picture? The effects of iconicity on toddlers' re-enactment from picture books. *Developmental Psychology, 42*, 1352–1357.

Simmons, D. R., Robertson, A. E., McKay, L. S., Toal, E., McAleer, P., & Pollick, F. E. (2009). Vision in autism spectrum disorders. *Vision Research, 49*, 2705–2739.

Simons, G. M. (1964). Comparisons of incipient music responses among very young twins and singletons. *Journal of Research in Music Education, 12*, 212–226.

Skoczenski, A. M., & Norcia, A. M. (2002). Late maturation of visual hyperacuity. *Psychological Science, 13*, 537–541.

Slater, A. (2001). Visual perception. In G. Bremner & A. Fogel (Eds), *Blackwell handbook of infant development* (pp. 5–34). Oxford: Blackwell.

Slater, A., & Butterworth, G. (1997). Perception of social stimuli: Face perception and imitation. In G. Bremner, A. Slater & G. Butterworth (Eds), *Infant development: Recent advances* (pp. 223–245). Hove, UK: Erlbaum.

Slater, A., Mattock, A., & Brown, E. (1990). Size constancy at birth: Newborn infants' responses to retinal and real size. *Journal of Experimental Child Psychology*, *49*, 314–322.

Slater, A., Morison, V., Town, C., & Rose, D. (1985). Movement perception and identity constancy in the new born baby. *British Journal of Developmental Psychology*, *3*, 211–220.

Slater, A., Rose, D., & Morison, V. (1984). New born infants' perception of similarities and differences between two and three dimensional stimuli. *British Journal of Developmental Psychology*, *2*, 287–294.

Søbstad, P. I. (1974). *Musikalsk utvikling hos barn i førskolealderen (Musical development in preschool age)*. Thesis, University of Oslo.

Søvik, N. (1993). Development of children's writing performance: Some educational implications. In A. F. Kalverboer, B. Hopkins & R. Geuze (Eds), *Motor development in early and later childhood: Longitudinal approaches* (pp. 229–241). Cambridge: Cambridge University Press.

Spelke, E. S. (1990). Principles of object perception. *Cognitive Science, 14*, 29–56.

Spelke, E. S., & Kinzler, K. D. (2007). Core knowledge. *Developmental Science*, *10*, 89–96.

Spelke, E. S., & Newport, E. L. (1998). Nativism, empiricism, and the development of knowledge. In W. Damon & R. M. Lerner (Eds), *Handbook of child psychology, Volume 1: Theoretical models of human development* (pp. 275–340). New York, NY: Wiley.

Spencer, P. E., & Marschark, M. (2010). *Evidence-based practice in educating deaf and hard-of-hearing students*. New York, NY: Oxford University Press.

Stadskleiv, K., Jahnsen, R., Andersen, G. L., & von Tetzchner, S. (2017). Neuropsychological profiles of children with cerebral palsy. *Developmental Neurorehabilitation*, *28*, 108–120.

Stadskleiv, K., von Tetzchner, S., Batorowicz, B., van Balkom, H., Dahlgren-Sandberg, A., & Renner, G. (2014). Investigating executive functions in children with severe speech and movement disorders using structured tasks. *Frontiers in Psychology*, *5*, 992.

Steiner, J. E., Glaser, D., Hawilo, M. E., & Berridge, K. C. (2001). Comparative expression of hedonic impact: Affective reactions to taste by human infants and other primates. *Neuroscience Biobehavioral Reviews*, *25*, 53–74.

Steinschneider, A., Lipton, E. L., & Richmond, J. B. (1966). Auditory sensitivity in the infant: Effect of intensity on cardiac and motor responsivity. *Child Development*, *1966*, 233–252.

Stevenson, J., Kreppner, J., Pimperton, H., Worsfold, S., & Kennedy, C. (2015). Emotional and behavioural difficulties in children and adolescents with hearing impairment: A systematic review and meta-analysis. *European Child and Adolescent Psychiatry, 24*, 477–496.

Super, C. M. (1981). Environmental effects on motor development: The case of "African infant precocity". *Developmental Medicine and Child Neurology, 18*, 561–567.

Thelen, E., & Smith, L. B. (1994). *A dynamic systems approach to the development of cognition and action.* London: MIT Press.

Trainor, L. J., & He, C. (2013). Auditory and musical development. In P. R. Zelazo (Ed.), *The Oxford handbook of developmental psychology, Volume 1: Body and mind* (pp. 310–337). New York, NY: Oxford University Press.

Trainor, L. J., & Trehub, S. E. (1994). Key membership and implied harmony in Western tonal music: Developmental perspectives. *Perception and Psychophysics, 56*, 125–132.

Trainor, L. J., & Unrau, A. J. (2012). Development of pitch and music perception. In L. Werner, R. R. Fay & A. N. Popper (Eds), *Springer handbook of auditory research: Human auditory development* (pp. 223–254). New York, NY: Springer.

Trehub, S. E., & Schellenberg, E. G. (1995). Music: Its relevance to infants. *Annals of Child Development, 11*, 1–24.

Troseth, G. L. (2003). Getting a clear picture: Young children's understanding of a televised image. *Developmental Science, 6*, 247–253.

Troseth, G. L., & DeLoache, J. S. (1998). The medium can obscure the message: Young children's understanding of video. *Child Development, 69*, 950–965.

Troseth, G. L., Pickard, M. E., & DeLoache, J. S. (2007). Young children's use of scale models: Testing an alternative to representational insight. *Developmental Science, 10*, 763–769.

Troseth, G. L., Pierroutsakos, S. L., & DeLoache, J. S. (2004). From the innocent to the intelligent eye: The early development of pictorial competence. *Advances in Child Development and Behavior, 32*, 1–35.

Tröster, H., & Brambring, M. (1992). Early social-emotional development in blind infants. *Child: Care, Health and Development, 18*, 207–227.

Turati, C., Valenza, E., Leo, I., & Simion, F. (2005). Three-month-olds' visual preference for faces and its underlying visual processing mechanisms. *Journal of Experimental Child Psychology, 90*, 255–273.

van Wieringen, A., & Wouters, J. (2015). What can we expect of normally-developing children implanted at a young age with respect to their auditory, linguistic and cognitive skills? *Hearing Research, 322*, 171–179.

Vervloed, M. P., van Dijk, R. J., Knoors, H., & van Dijk, J. P. (2006). Interaction between the teacher and the congenitally deafblind child. *American Annals of the Deaf, 151*, 336–344.

von Hofsten, C. (1993). Studying the development of goaldirected behaviour. In A. F. Kalverboer, B. Hopkins & R. Geuze (Eds), *Motor development in early and later childhood: Longitudinal approaches* (pp. 109–124). Cambridge: Cambridge University Press.

von Hofsten, C. (2004). An action perspective on motor development. *Trends in Cognitive Sciences, 8,* 266–272.

von Hofsten, C. (2007). Action in development. *Developmental Science, 10,* 54–60.

von Hofsten, O., von Hofsten, C., Sulutvedt, U., Laeng, B., Brennen, T., & Magnussen, S. (2014). Simulating newborn face perception. *Journal of Vision, 14,* 16.

von Tetzchner, S., Elmerskog, B., Tøssebro, A.-G., & Rokne, S. (Eds) (2019). Juvenile Neuronal Ceroid Lipofuscinosis, Childhood Dementia and Education. Trondheim, Norway: Snøfugl. Free download: https://www.statped.no/larings ressurser/syn/juvenile-neuronal-ceroid-lipofuscinosis-childhood-dementia-and-education/

Want, S. C., Pascalis, O., Coleman, M., & Blades, M. (2003). Recognizing people from the inner or outer parts of their faces: Developmental data concerning "unfamiliar" faces. *British Journal of Developmental Psychology, 21,* 125–135.

Waterhouse, L. (2006a). Multiple intelligences, the Mozart effect, and emotional intelligence: A critical review. *Educational Psychologist, 41,* 207–225.

Waterhouse, L. (2006b). Inadequate evidence for multiple intelligences, Mozart effect, and emotional intelligence theories. *Educational Psychologist, 41,* 247–255.

Webster, A., & Roe, J. (1998). *Children with visual impairments. Social interaction, language and learning.* New York, NY: Routledge.

Werner, E. E. (2012). Children and war: Risk, resilience, and recovery. *Development and Psychopathology, 24,* 553–558.

Werner, H. (1961). *Comparative psychology of mental development.* New York, NY: Science Editions.

Werner, L. A. (2007). Issues in human auditory development. *Journal of Communication Disorders, 40,* 275–283.

Wertheimer, M. (1961). Psychomotor coordination of auditory and visual space at birth. *Science, 134,* 1692.

White, S., Milne, E., Rosen, S., Hansen, P., Swettenham, J., Frith, U., & Ramus, F. (2006). The role of sensorimotor impairments in dyslexia: A multiple case study of dyslexic children. *Developmental Science, 9,* 237–255.

Wilson, B., & Wilson, M. (1977). An iconoclastic view of the imagery sources in the drawings of young people. *Art Education, 30,* 5–11.

Winner, E. (2006). Development in the arts: Drawing and music. In W. Damon, R. M. Lerner, D. Kuhn & R. S. Siegler (Eds), *Handbook of child psychology, Sixth edition, Volume 2: Cognition, perception and language* (pp. 859–904). New York, NY: Wiley.

Woll, B., & Morgan, G. (2012). Language impairments in the development of sign: Do they reside in a specific modality or are they modality independent deficits? *Bilingualism: Language and Cognition, 15,* 75–87.

Wong, S., Chan, K., Wong, V., & Wong, W. (2002). Use of chopsticks in Chinese children. *Child Care, Health and Development, 28,* 157–161.

Xia, F. (2014). *Finding Monet.* Shanghai: Changning Special Education Center.

Xu, F., & Carey, S. (1996). Infants' metaphysics: The case of numerical identity. *Cognitive Psychology, 30,* 111–153.

Yonas, A., Elieff, C. A., & Arterberry, M. E. (2002). Emergence of sensitivity to pictorial depth cues: Charting development in individual infants. *Infant Behavior and Development, 25,* 495–514.

Yoshinaga-Itano, C. (2013). Principles and guidelines for early intervention after confirmation that a child is deaf or hard of hearing. *Journal of Deaf Studies and Deaf Education, 19,* 143–175.

Zihl, J., & Dutton, G. N. (2015). *Cerebral visual impairment in children.* Wien, Austria: Springer.

Index

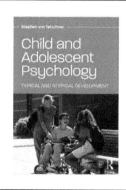

The **Topics from Child and Adolescent Psychology Series** is drawn from Stephen von Tetzchner's comprehensive textbook for all students of developmental psychology, *Child and Adolescent Psychology: Typical and Atypical Development*

Table of Contents

Praise for *Child and Adolescent Psychology: Typical and Atypical Development*

'An extensive overview of the field of developmental psychology. It illustrates how knowledge about typical and atypical development can be integrated and used to highlight fundamental processes of human growth and maturation.'

Dr. John Coleman, *PhD, OBE, UK*

'A broad panoply of understandings of development from a wide diversity of perspectives and disciplines, spanning all the key areas, and forming a comprehensive, detailed and extremely useful text for students and practitioners alike.'

Dr. Graham Music, *Consultant Psychotherapist,*
Tavistock Clinic London, UK

'An extraordinary blend of depth of scholarship with a lucid, and engaging, writing style. Its coverage is impressive . . . Both new and advanced students will love the coverage of this text.'

Professor Joseph Campos, *University of California, USA*

'Encyclopedic breadth combined with an unerring eye for the central research across developmental psychology, particularly for the period of its explosive growth since the 1960s. Both a text and a reference work, this will be the go-to resource for any teacher, researcher or student of the discipline for the foreseeable future.'

Professor Andy Lock, *University of Lisbon, Portugal*

It is accompanied by a companion website featuring chapter summaries, glossary, quizzes and instructor resources.

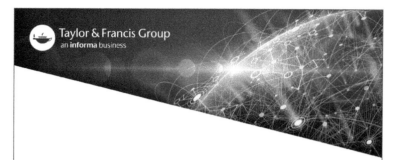